The Whimsical Alphabet Garden

By Vonda Weikert

authorHOUSE

AuthorHouse™
1663 Liberty Drive
Bloomington, IN 47403
www.authorhouse.com
Phone: 1-800-839-8640

First published by AuthorHouse 3/17/2011

ISBN: 978-1-4567-5281-1 (sc)

Library of Congress Control Number: 2011903967

Printed in the United States of America

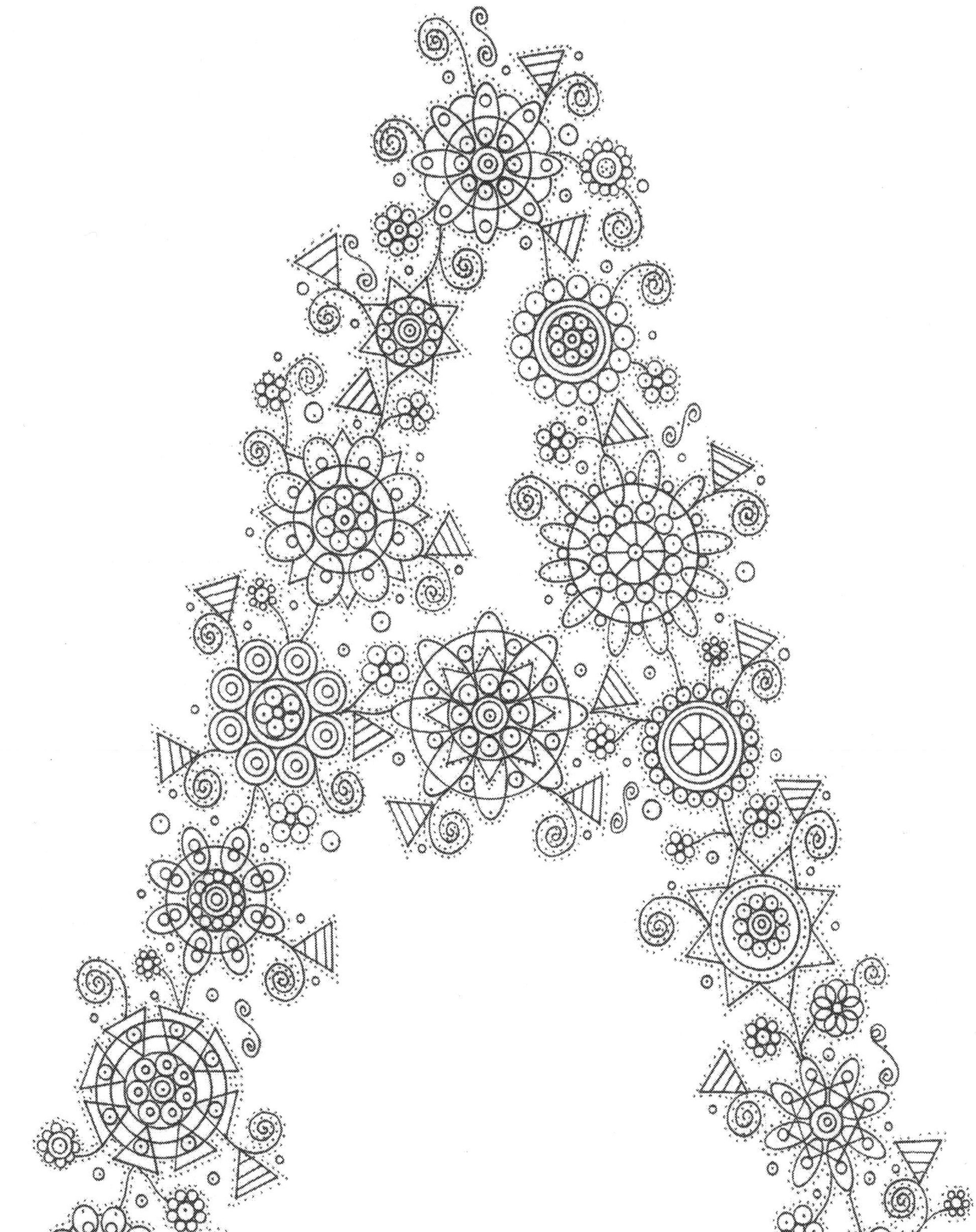

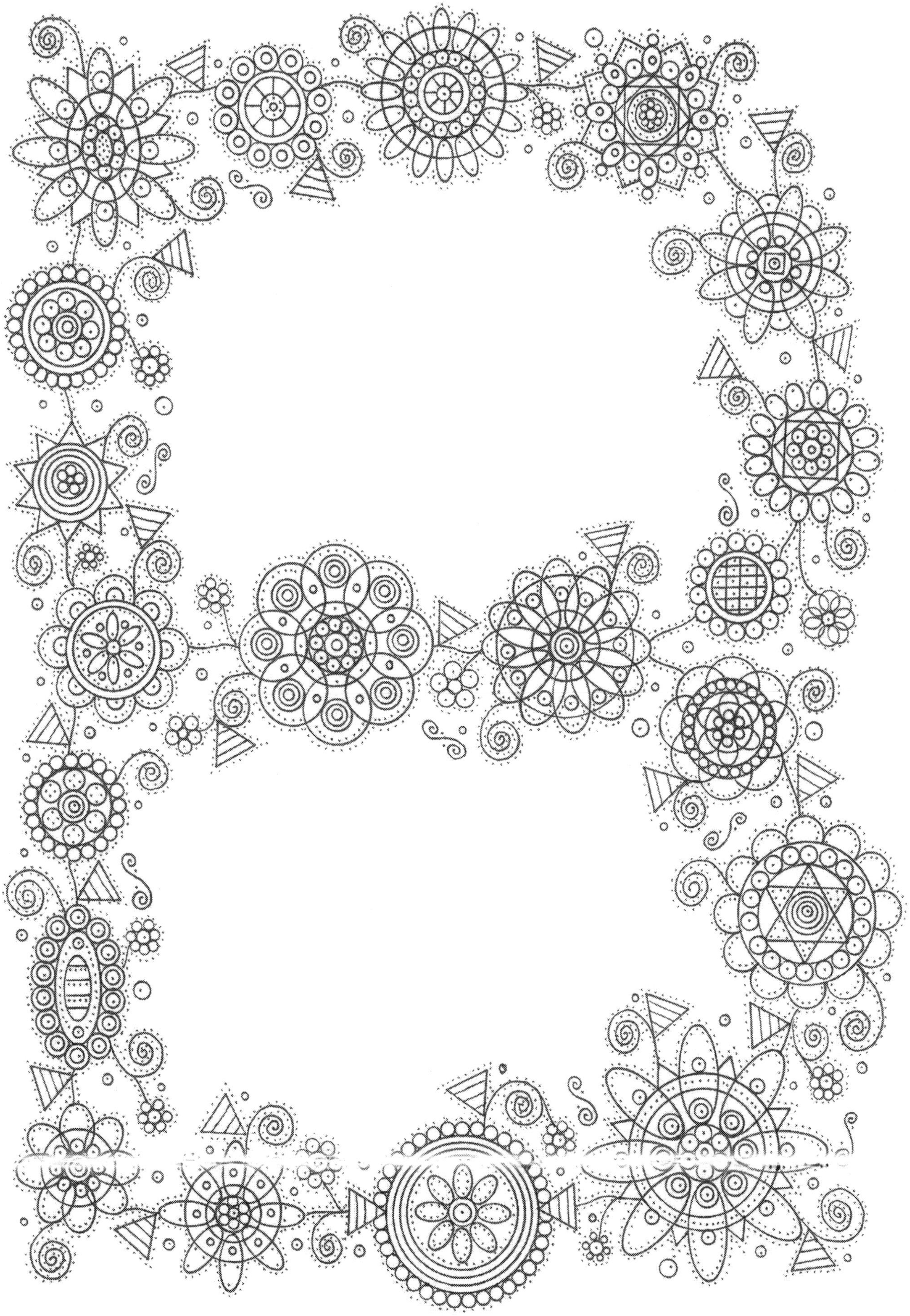

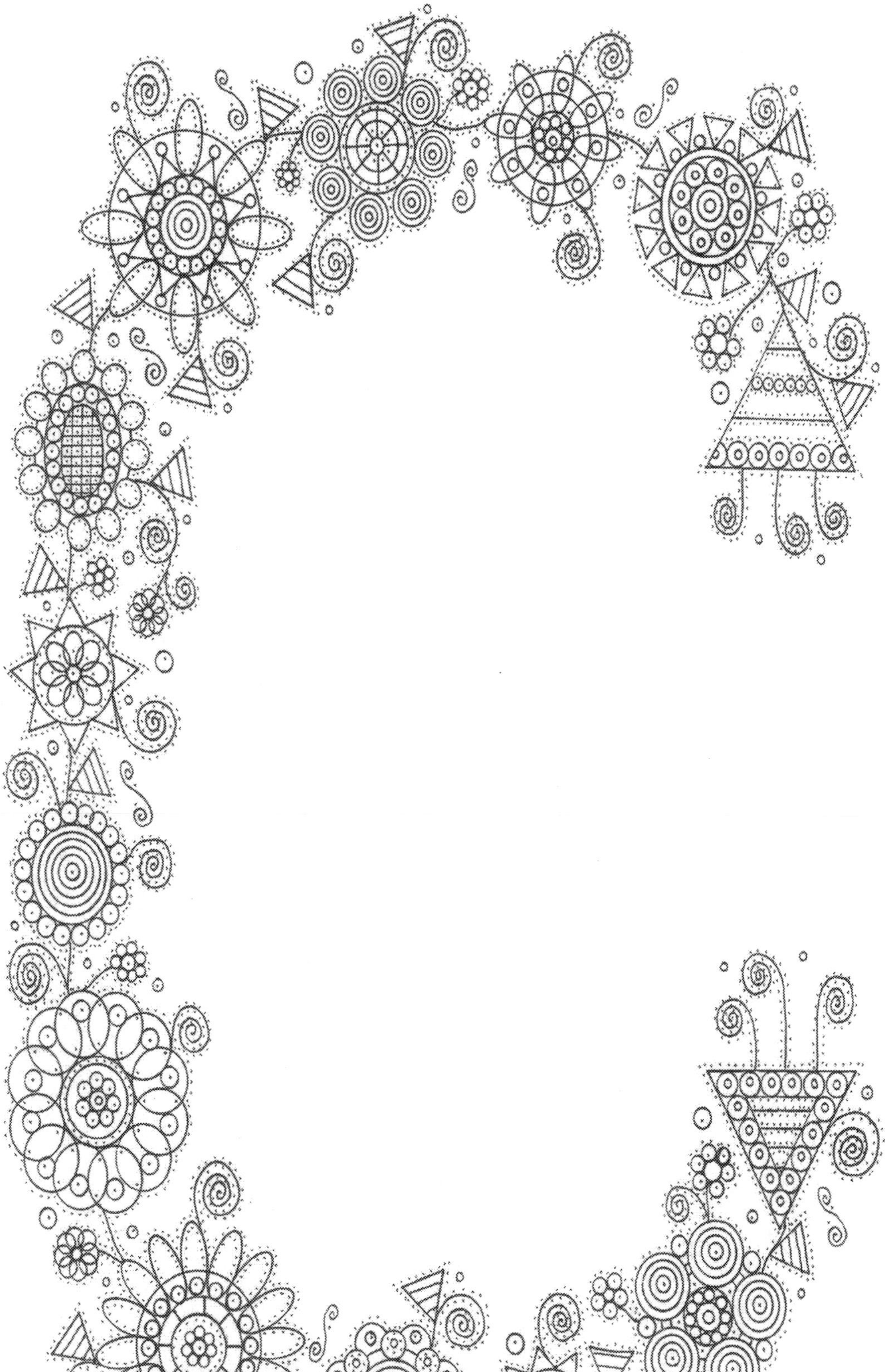

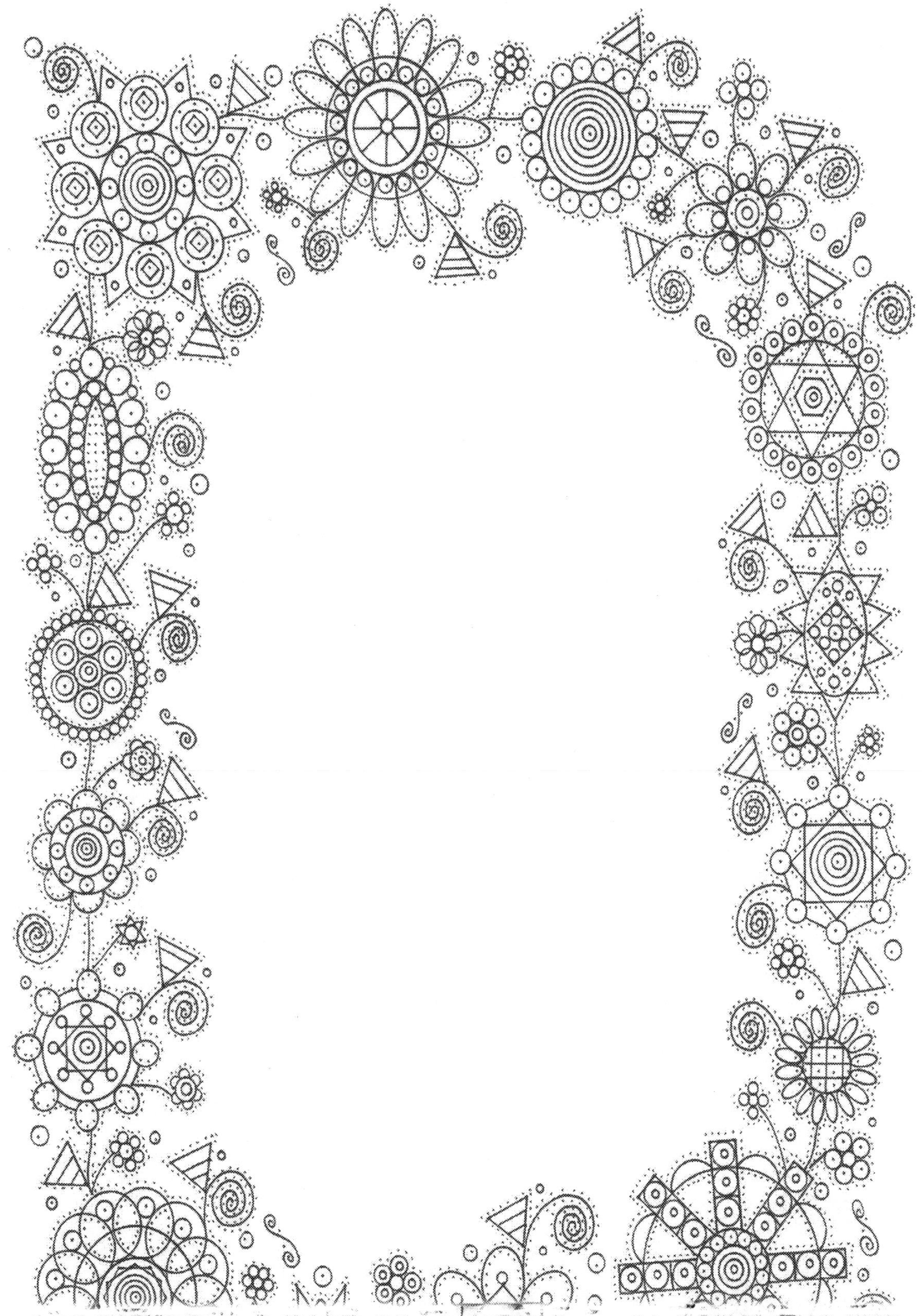

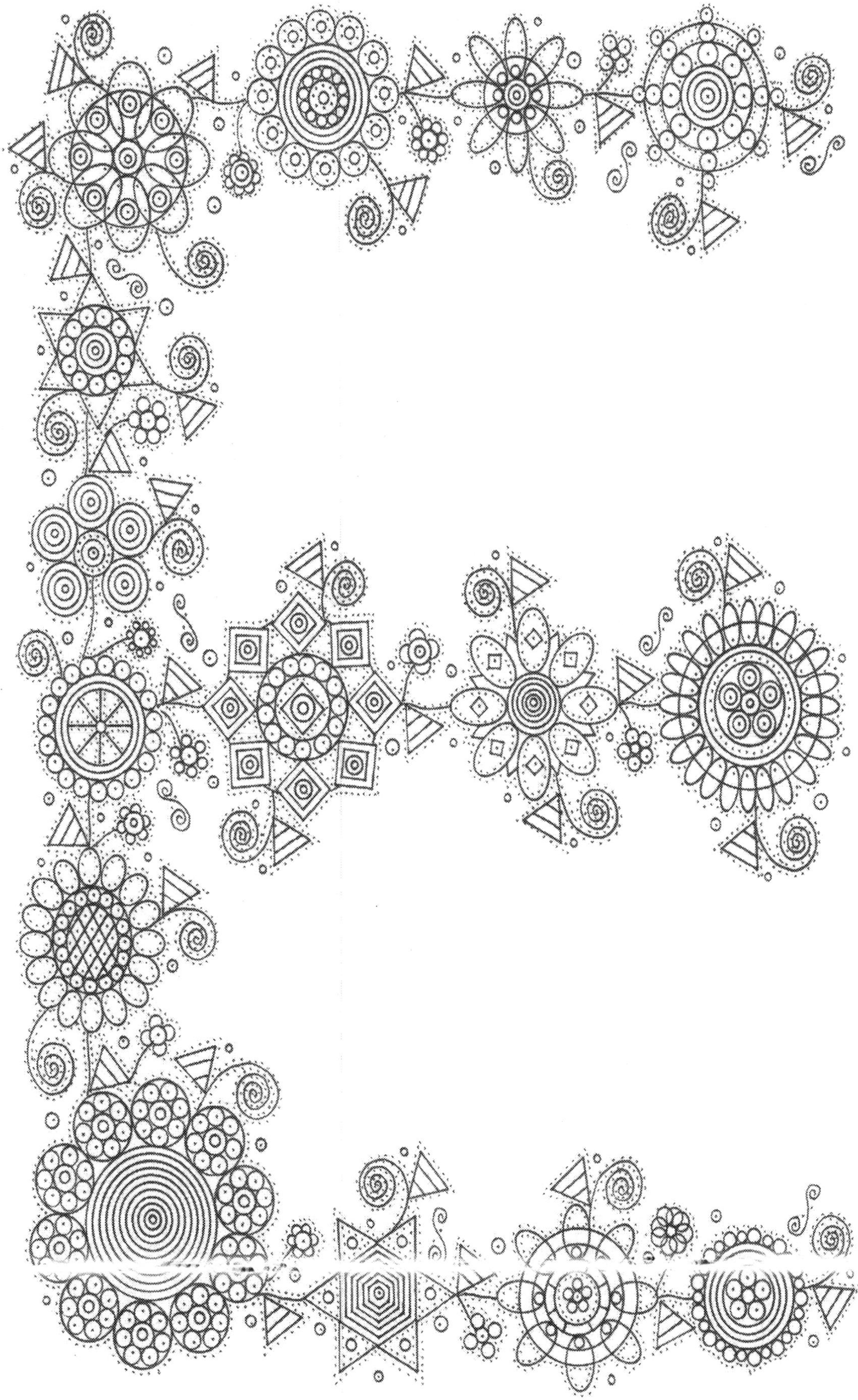

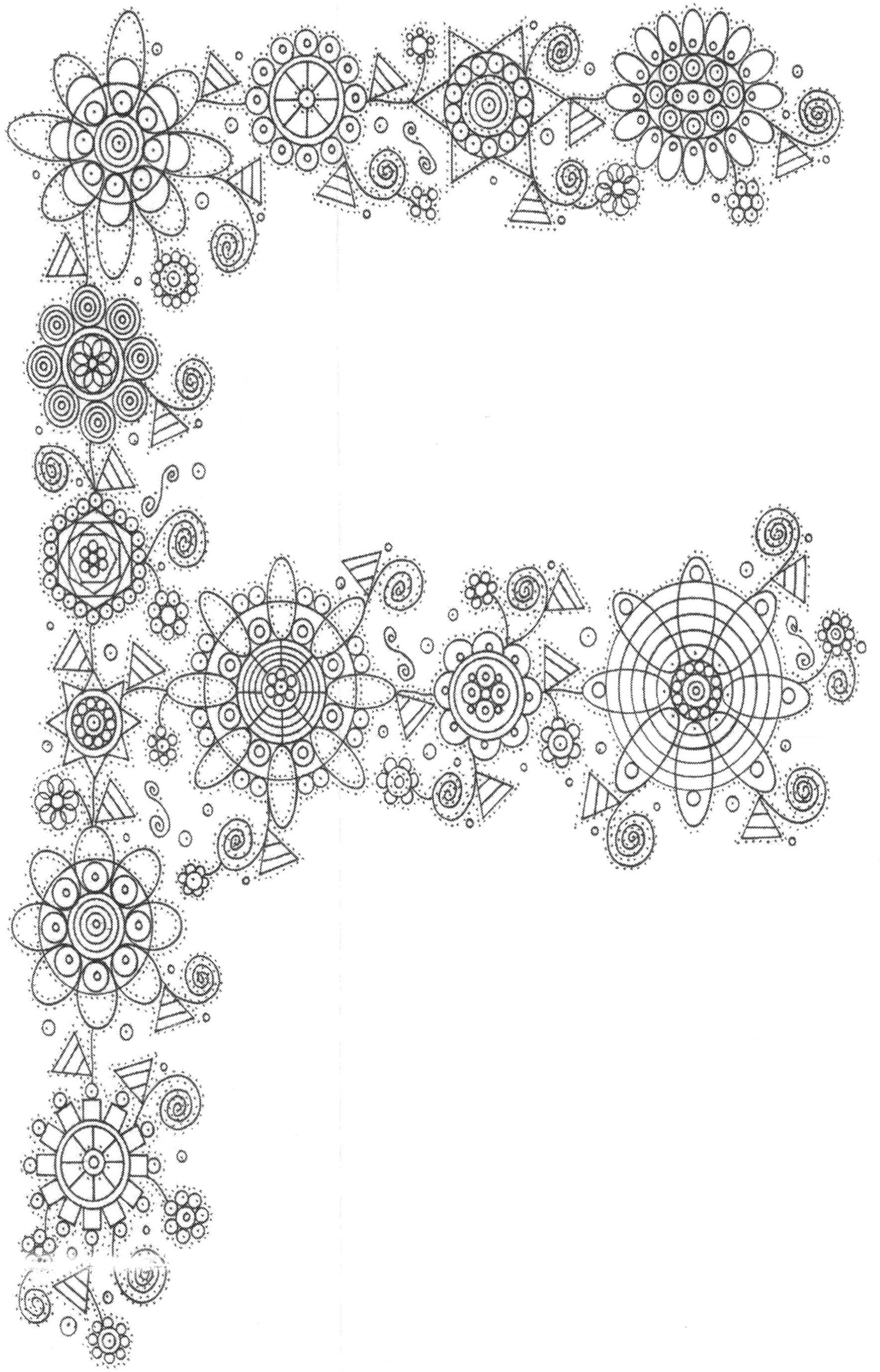

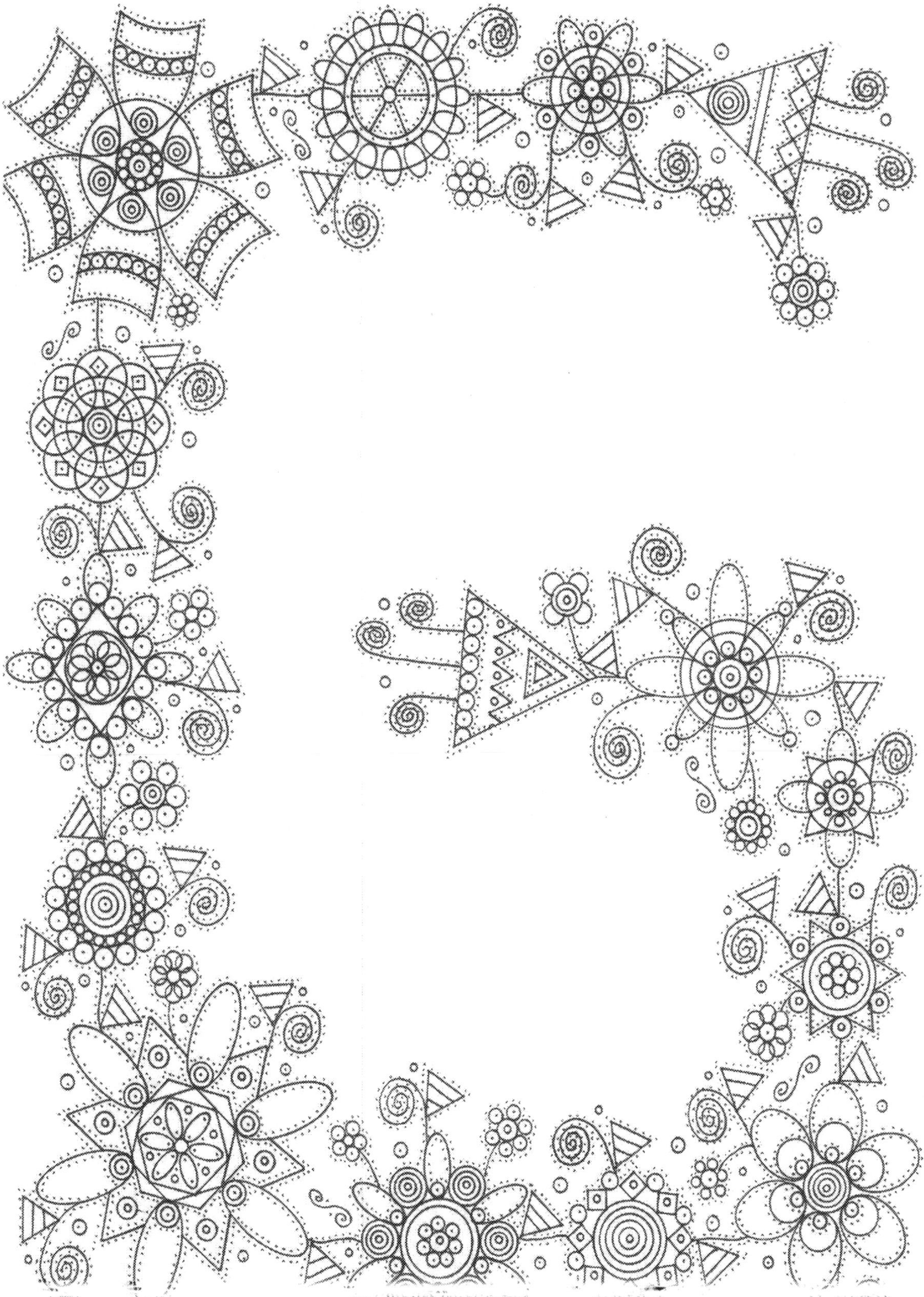

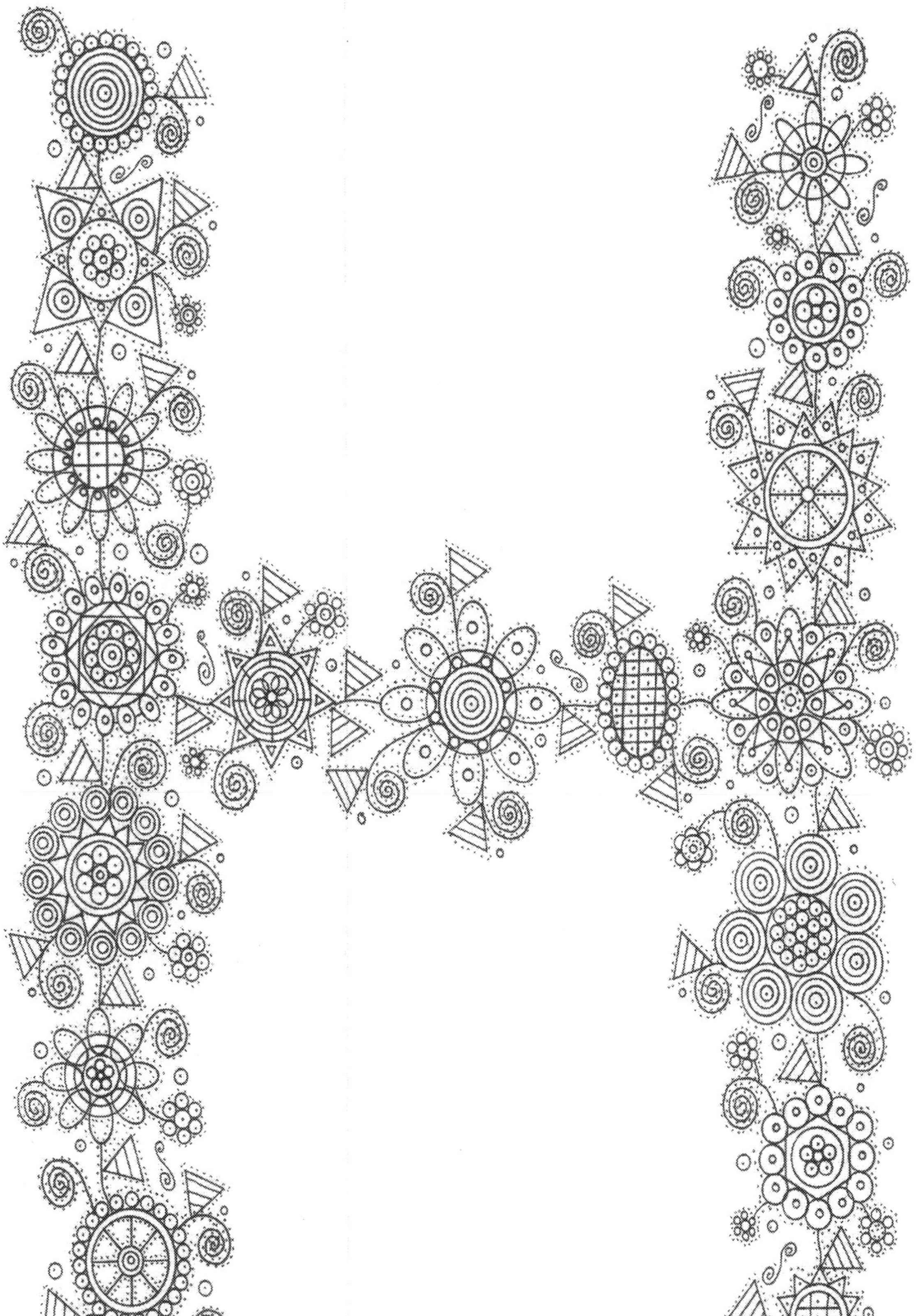

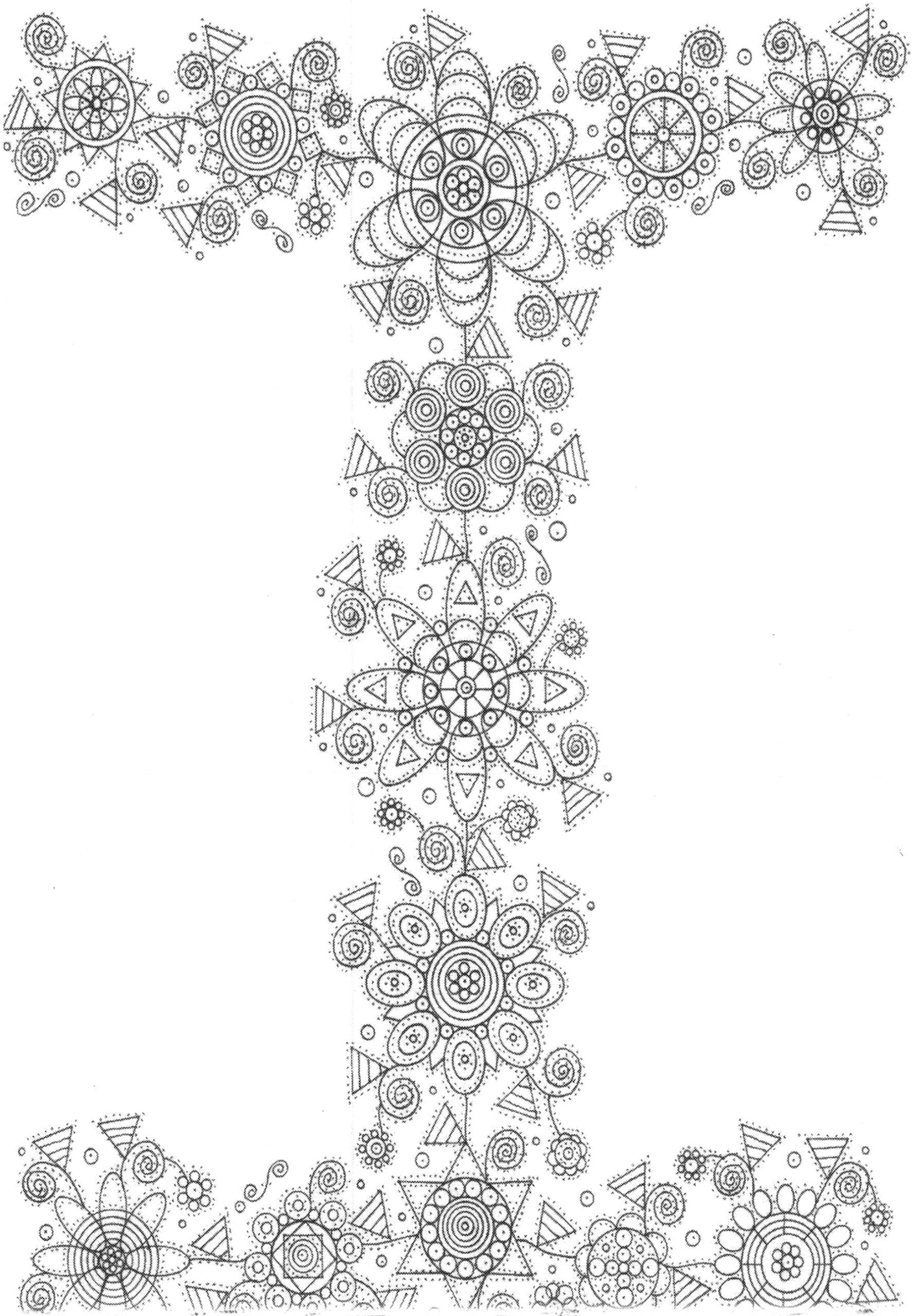

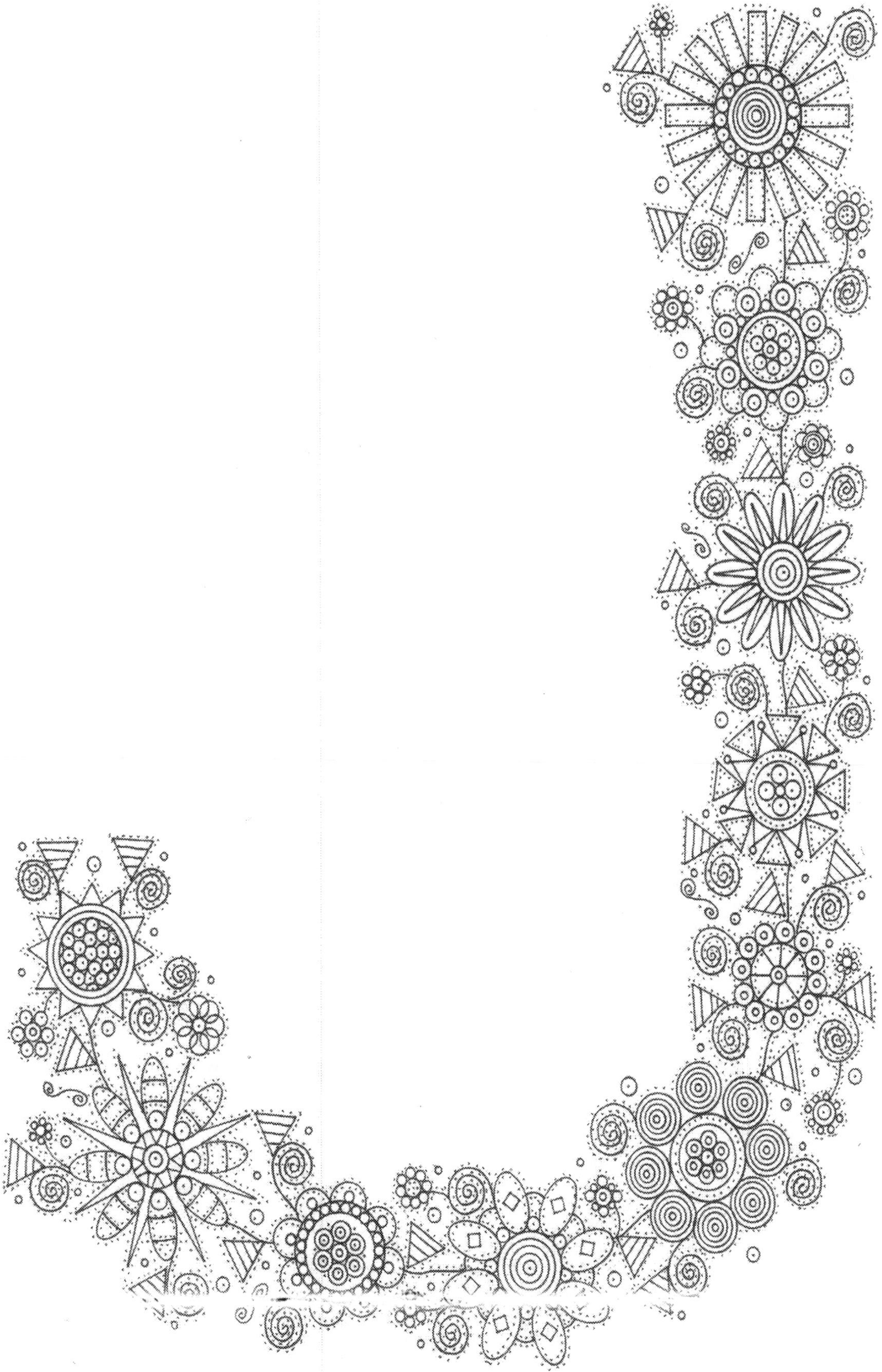

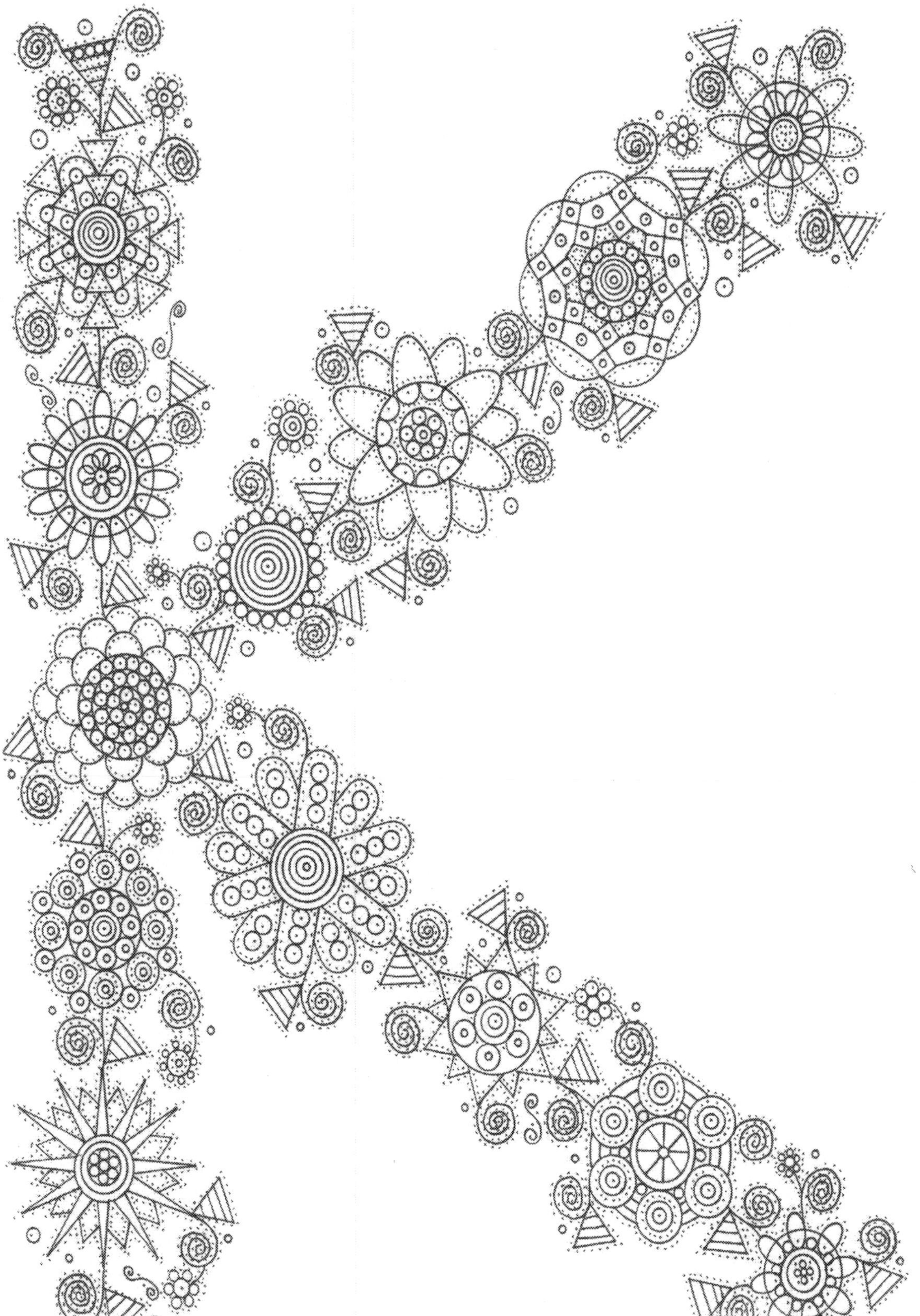

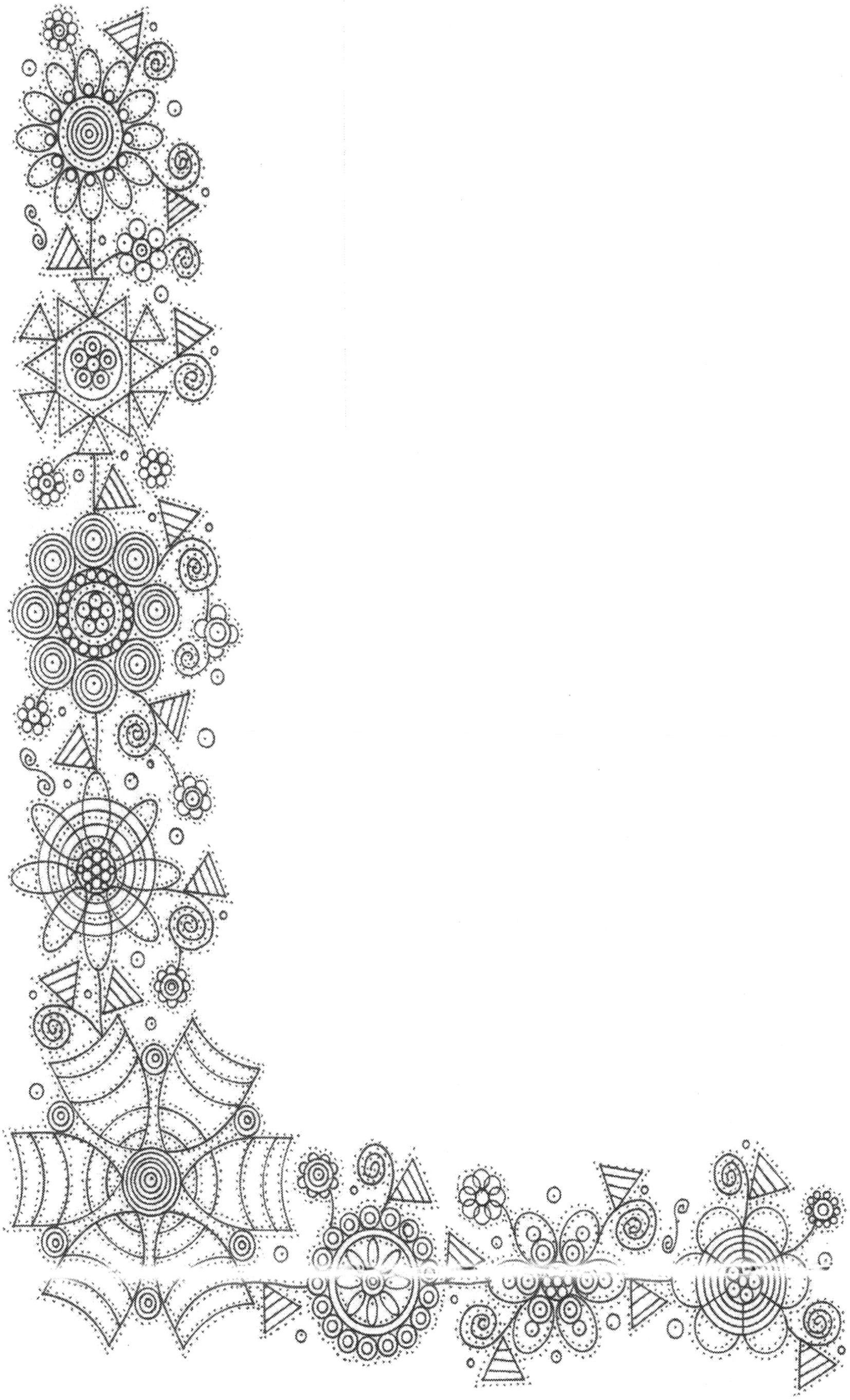

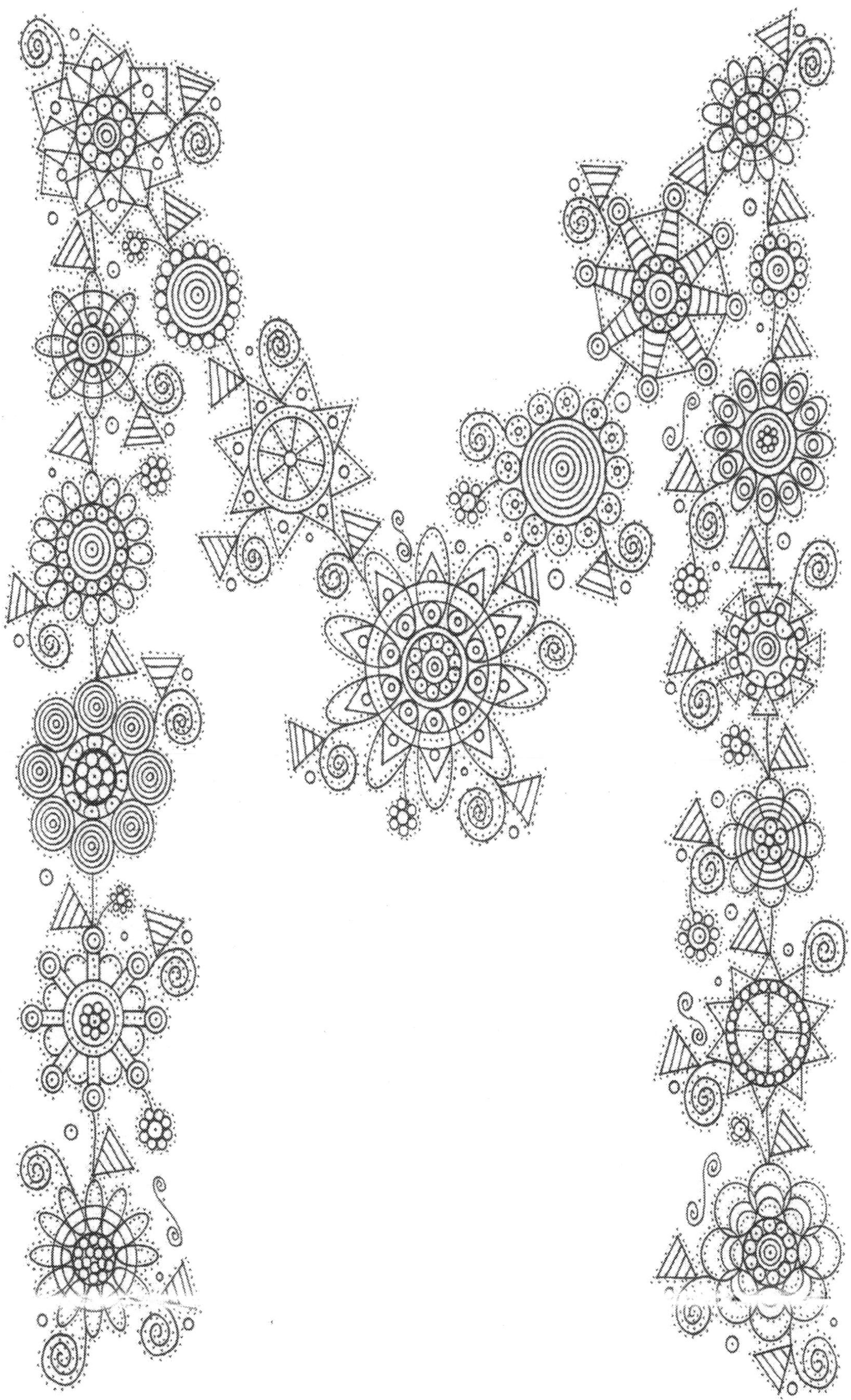

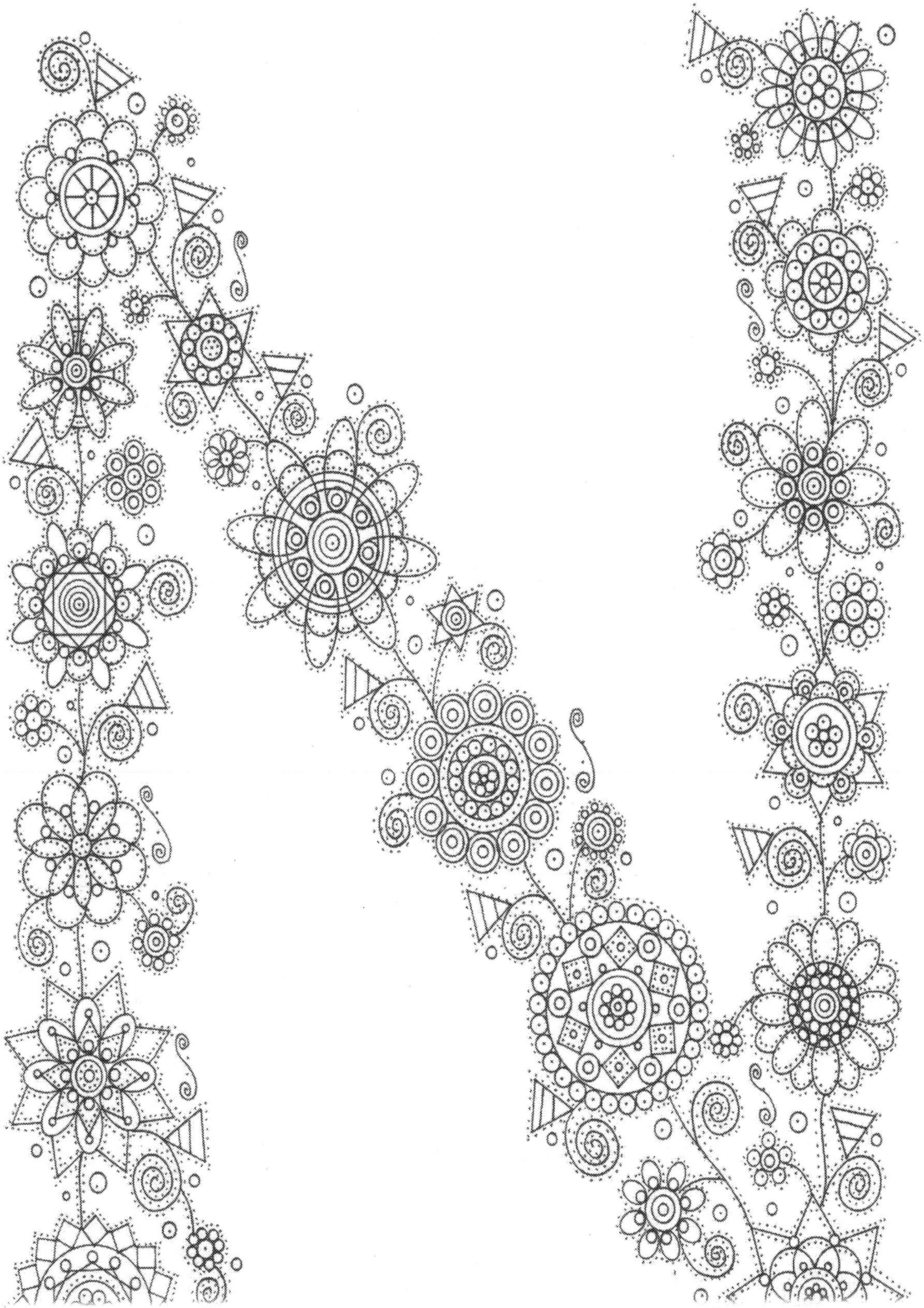

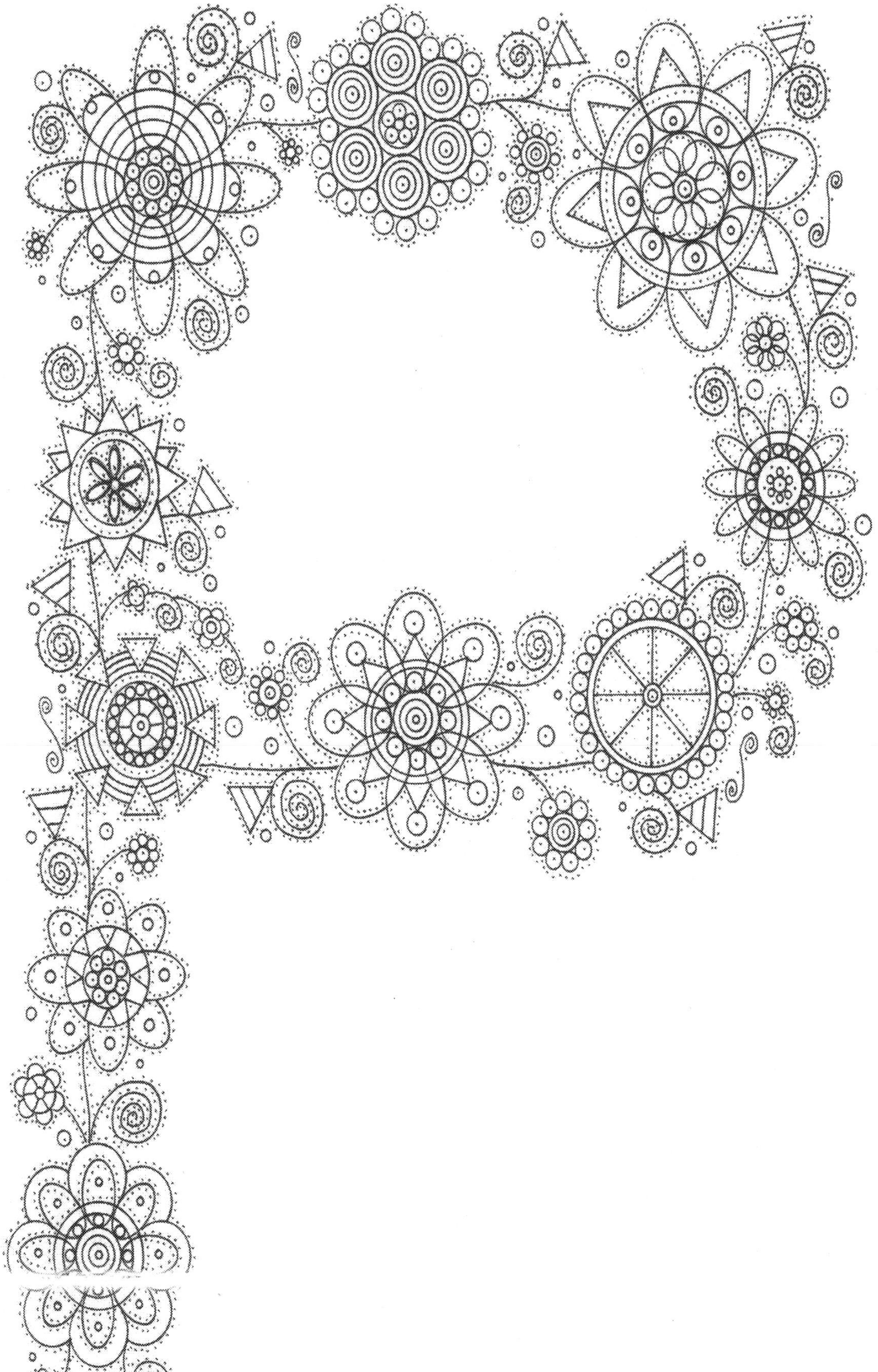

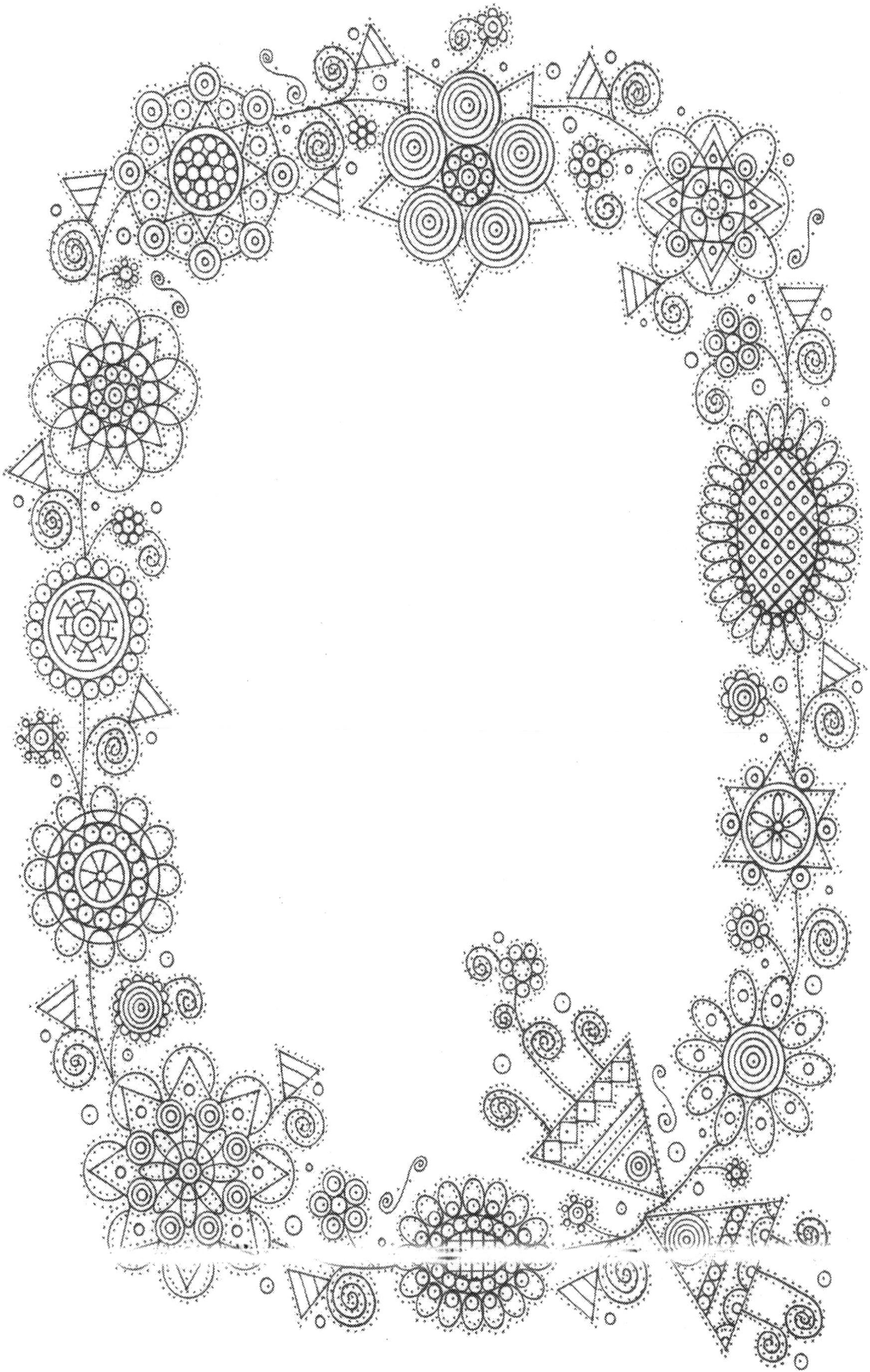

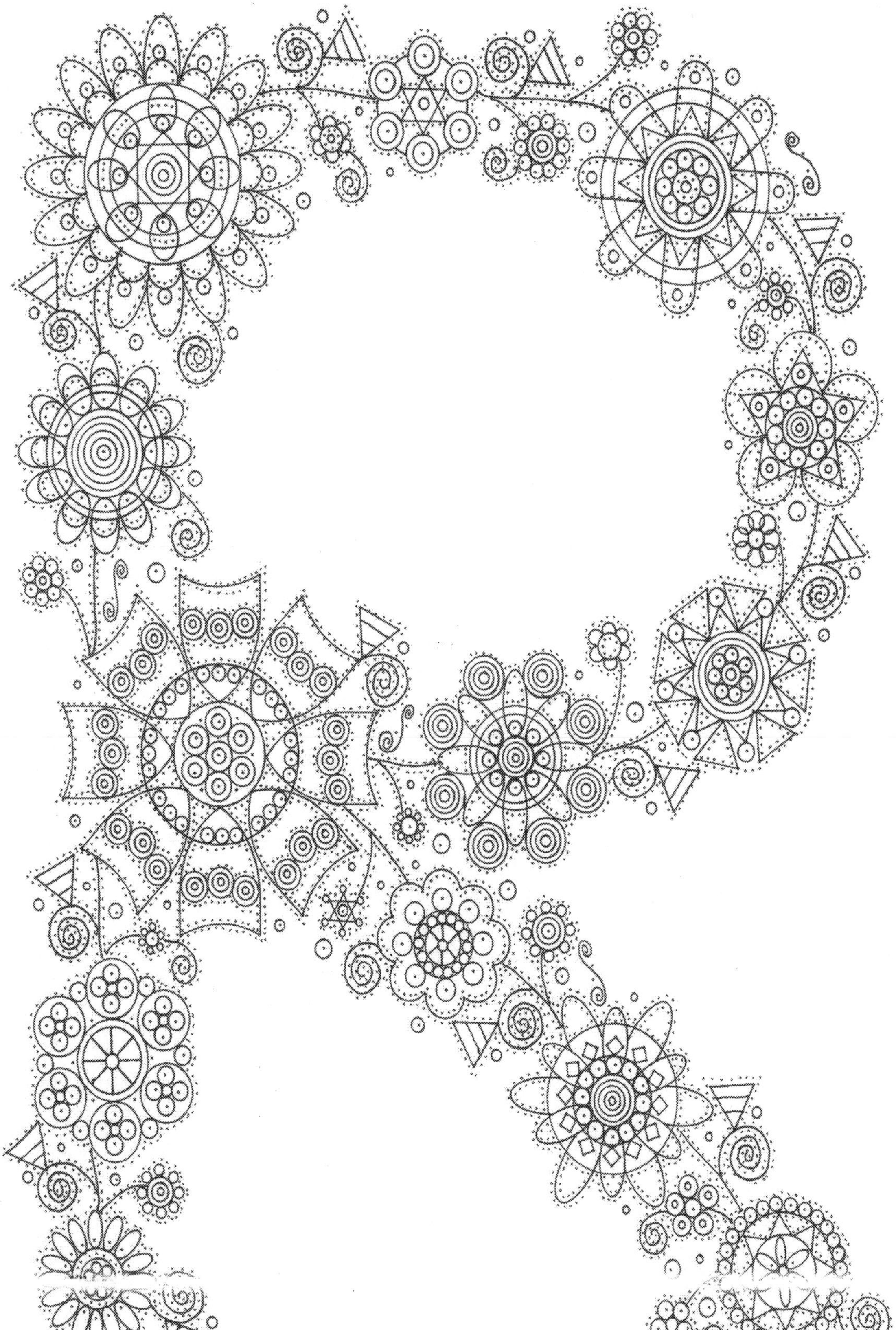

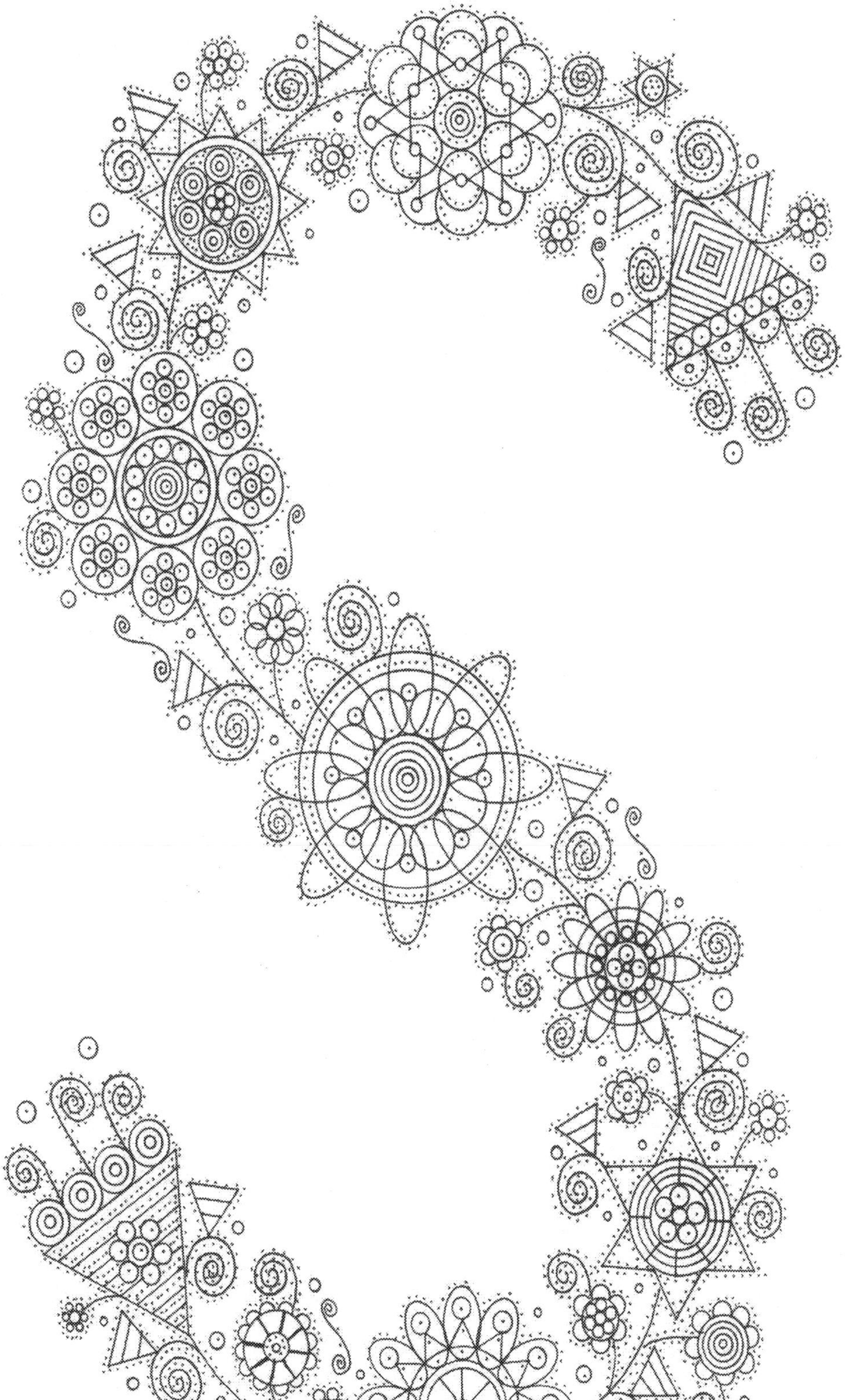

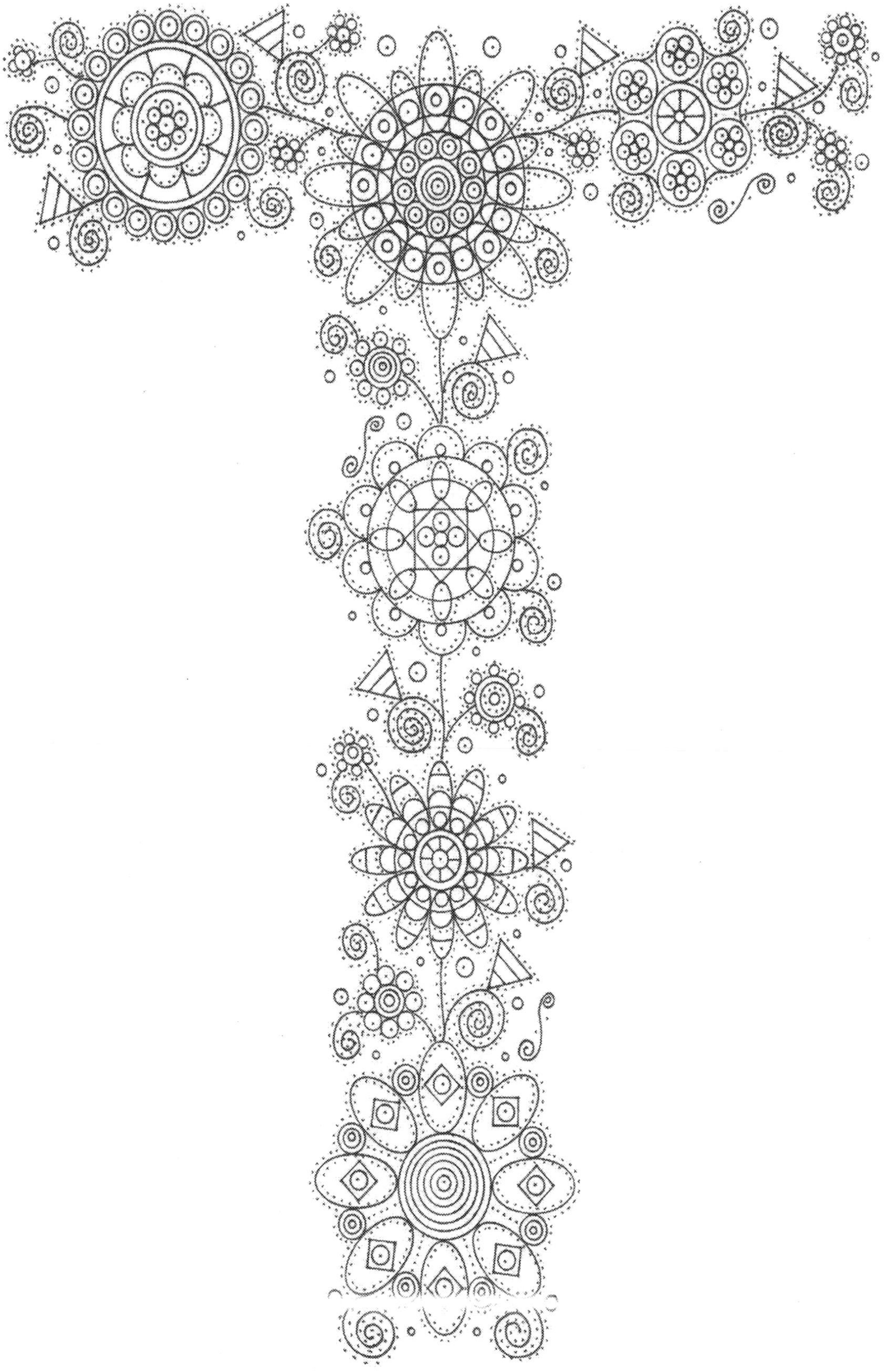

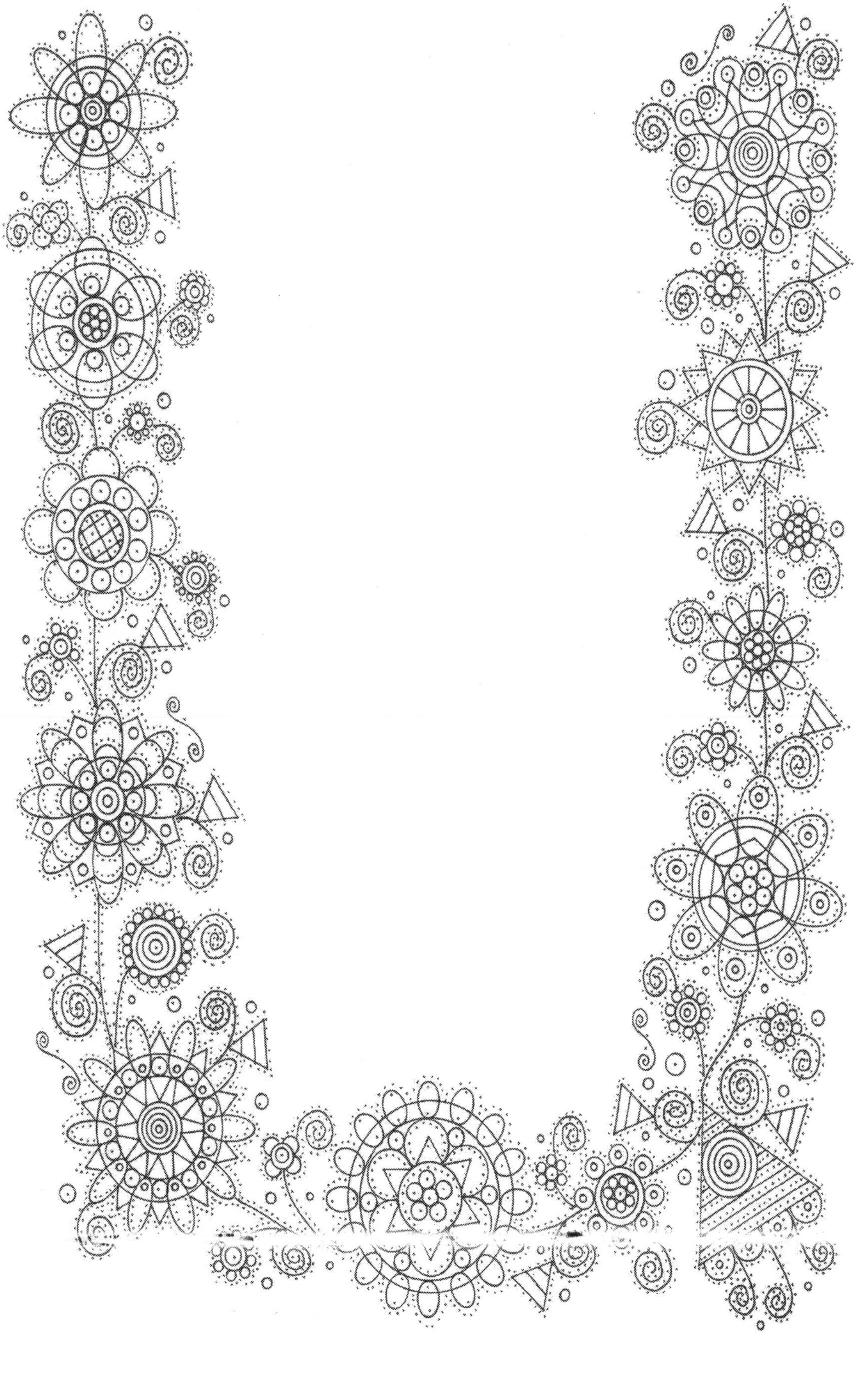

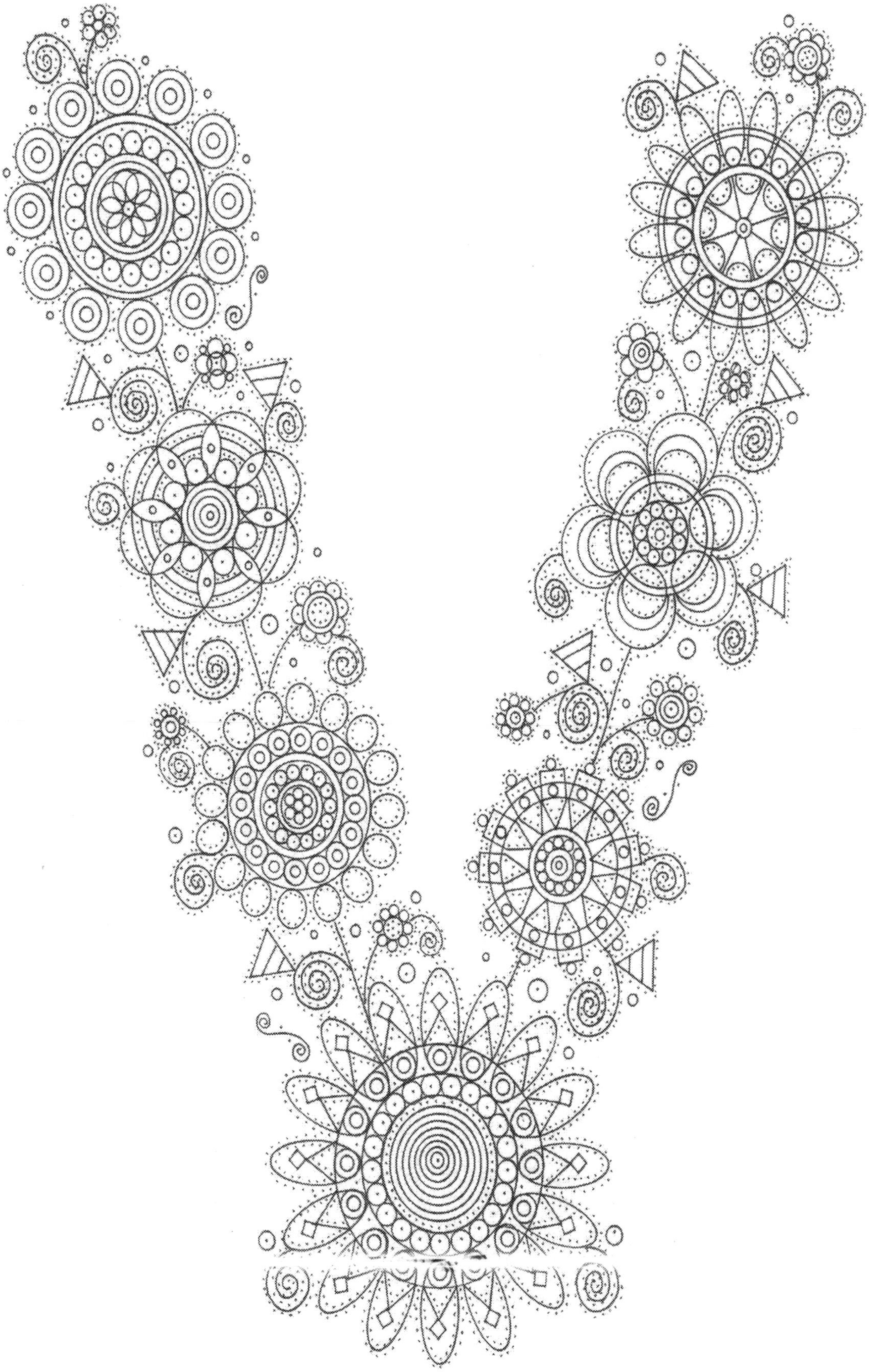

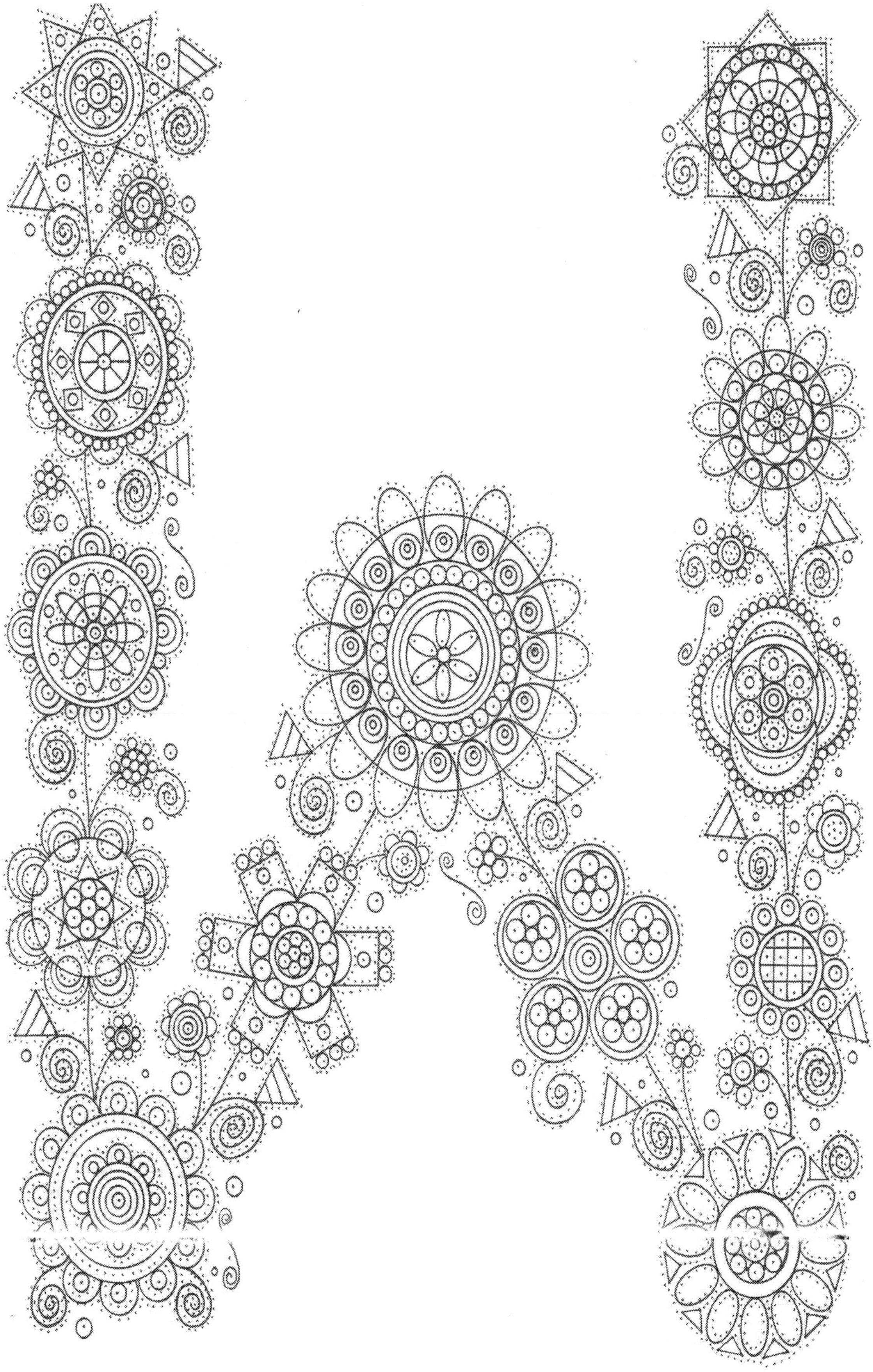

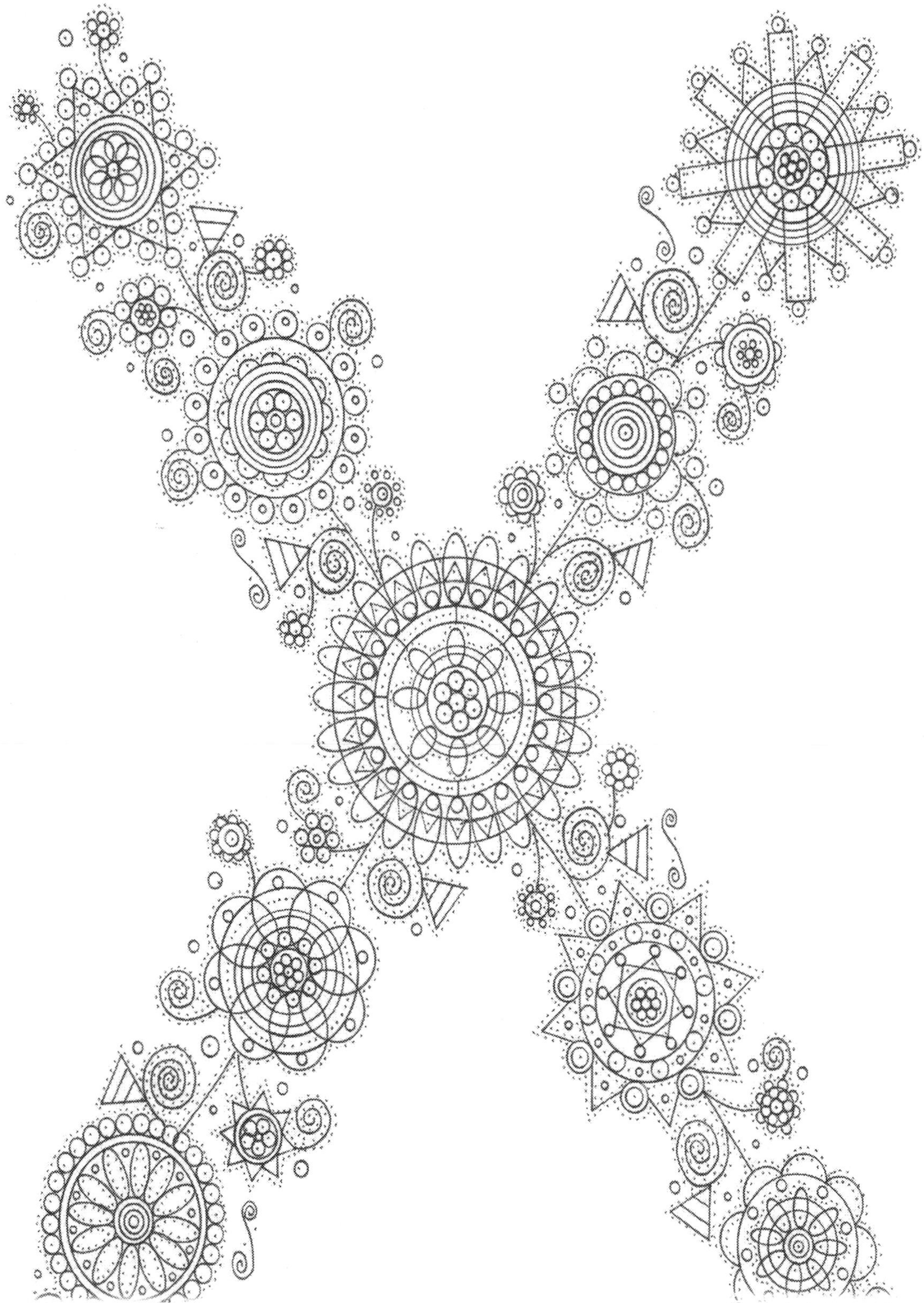

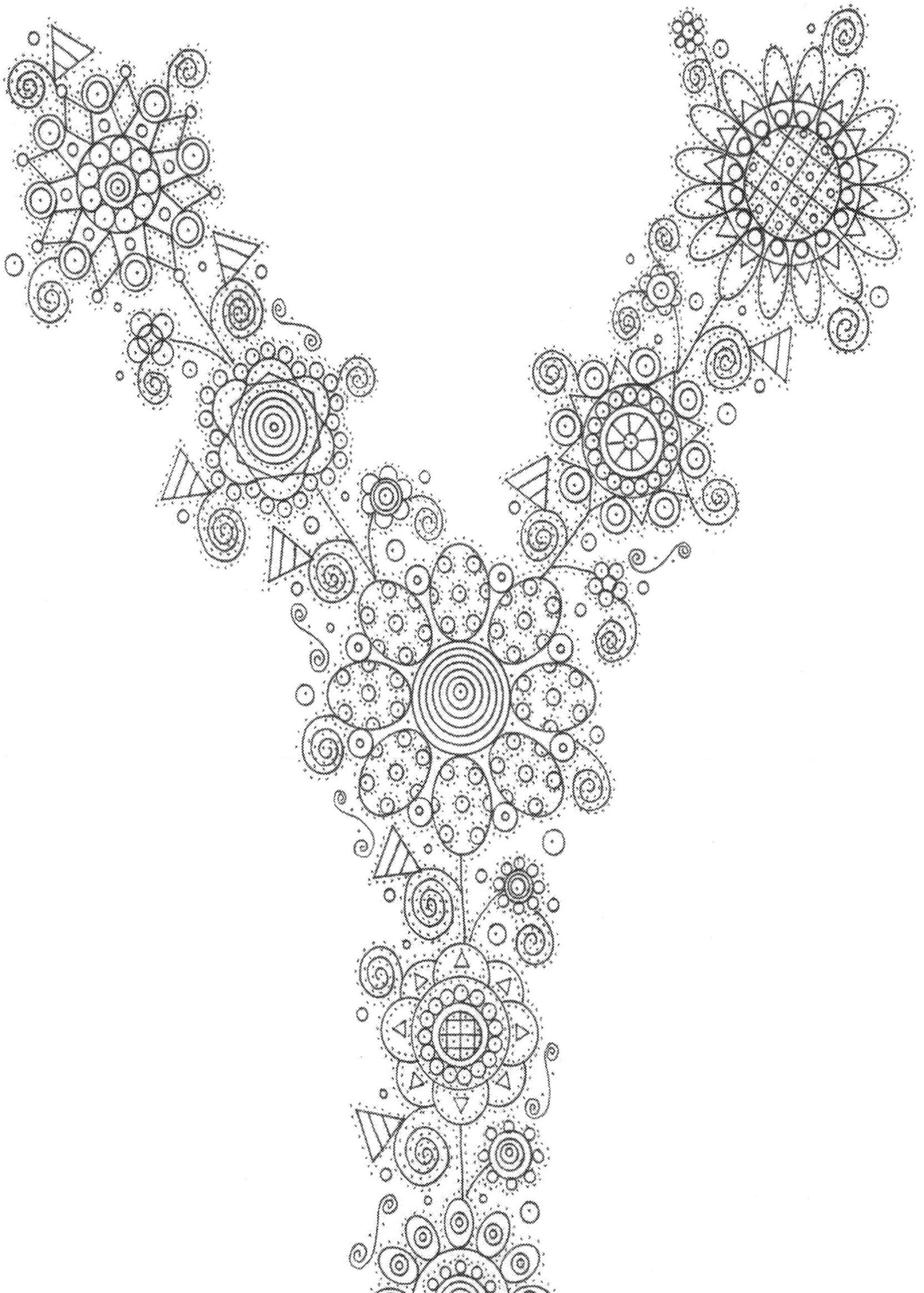

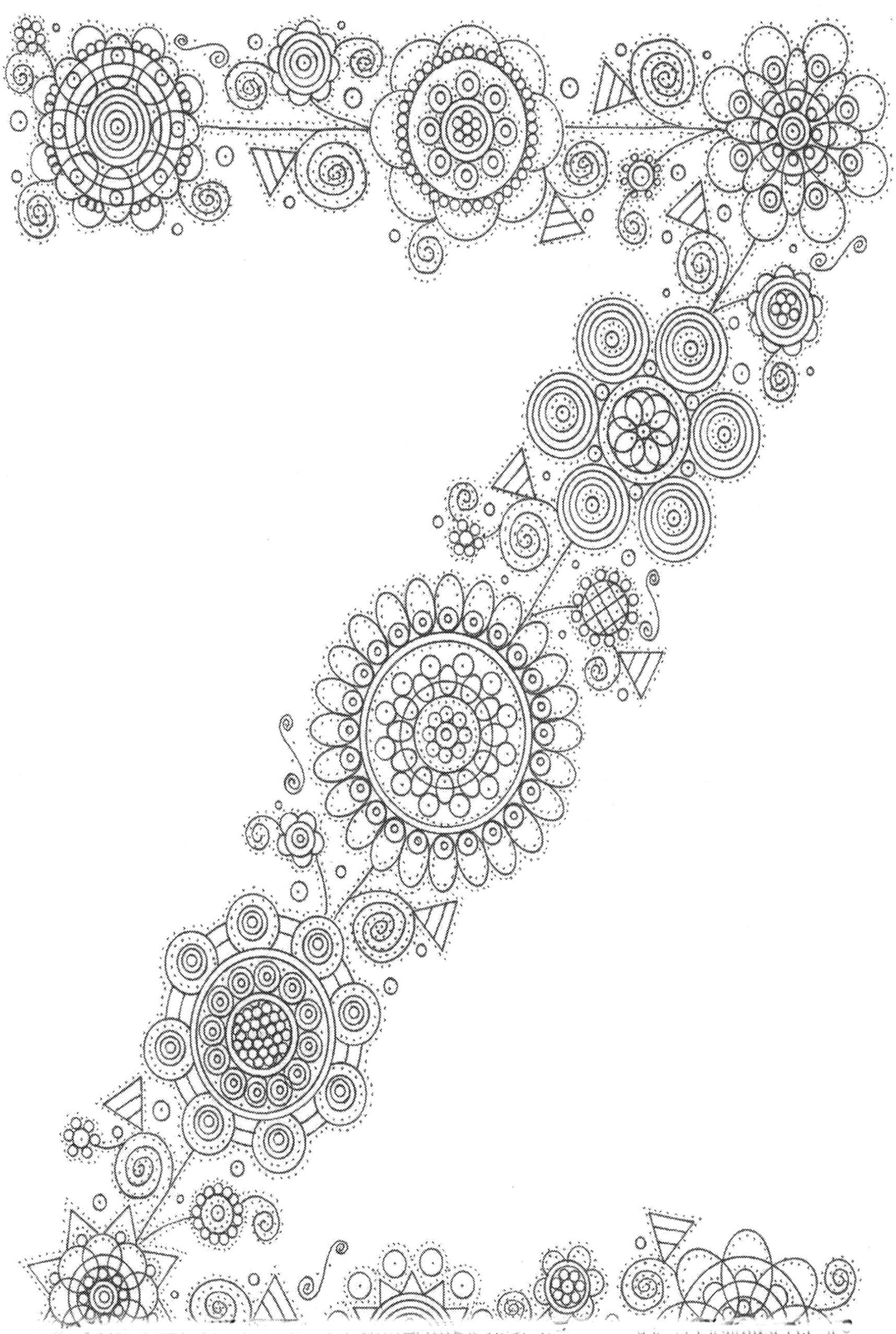

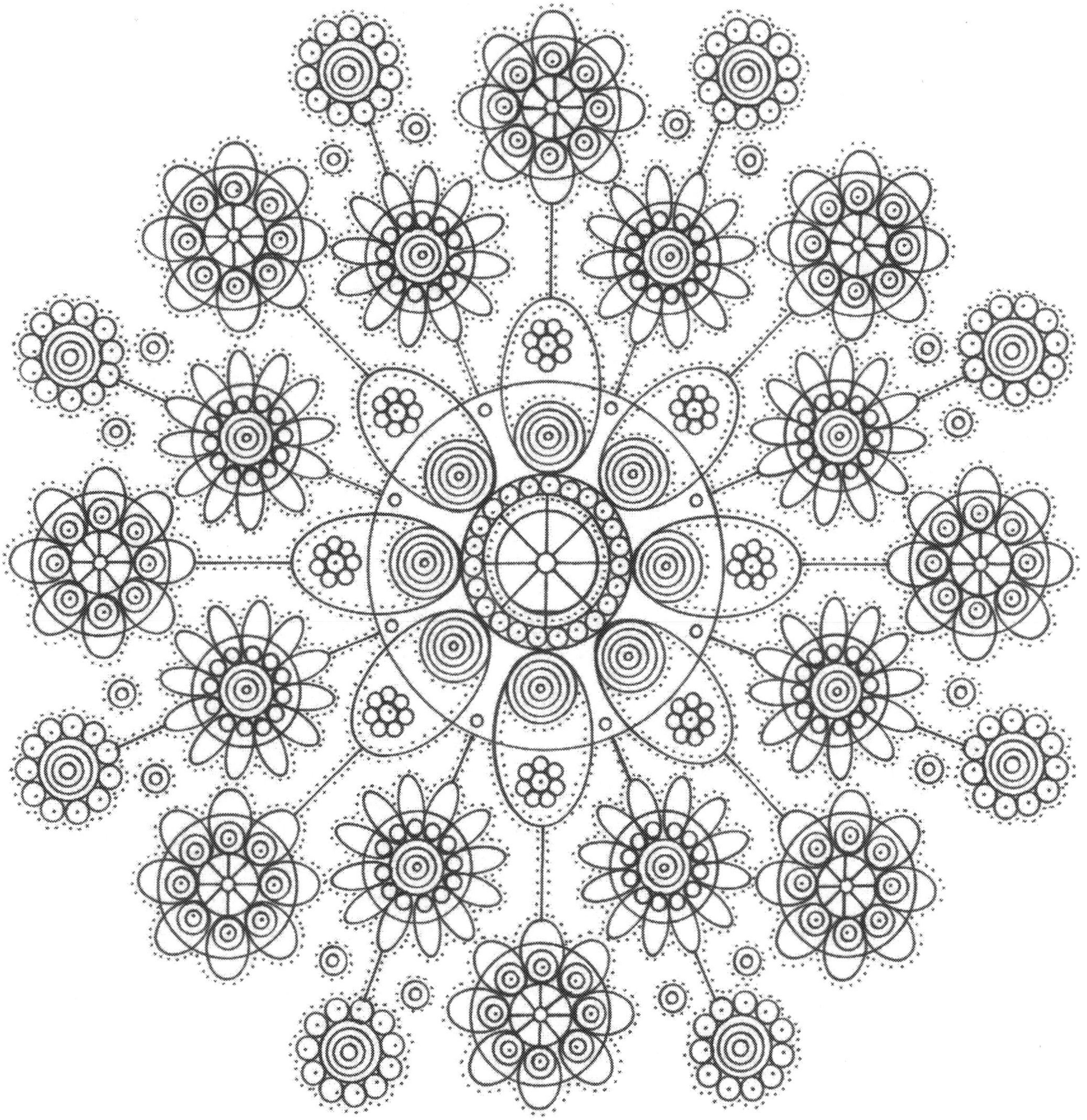

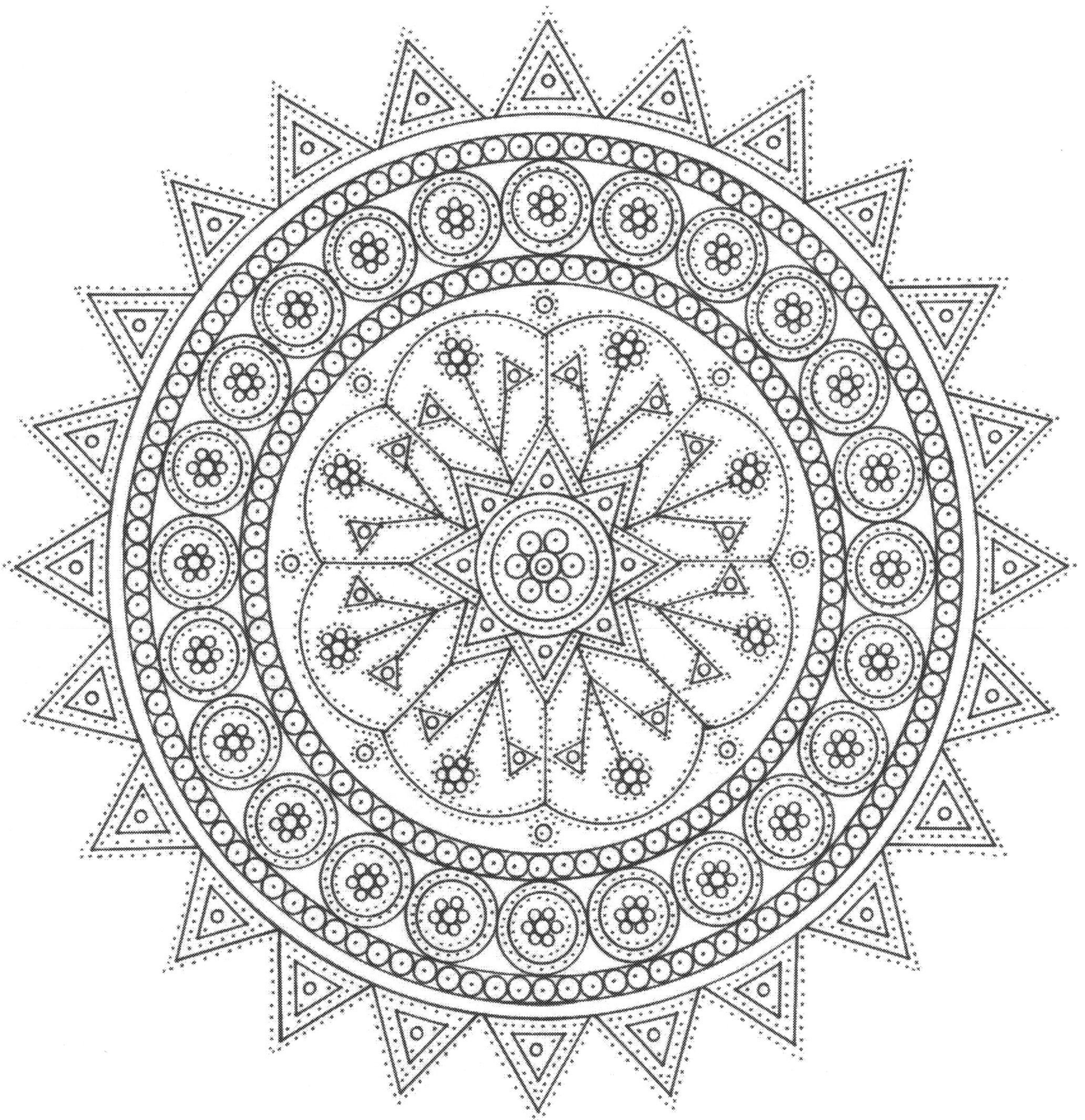

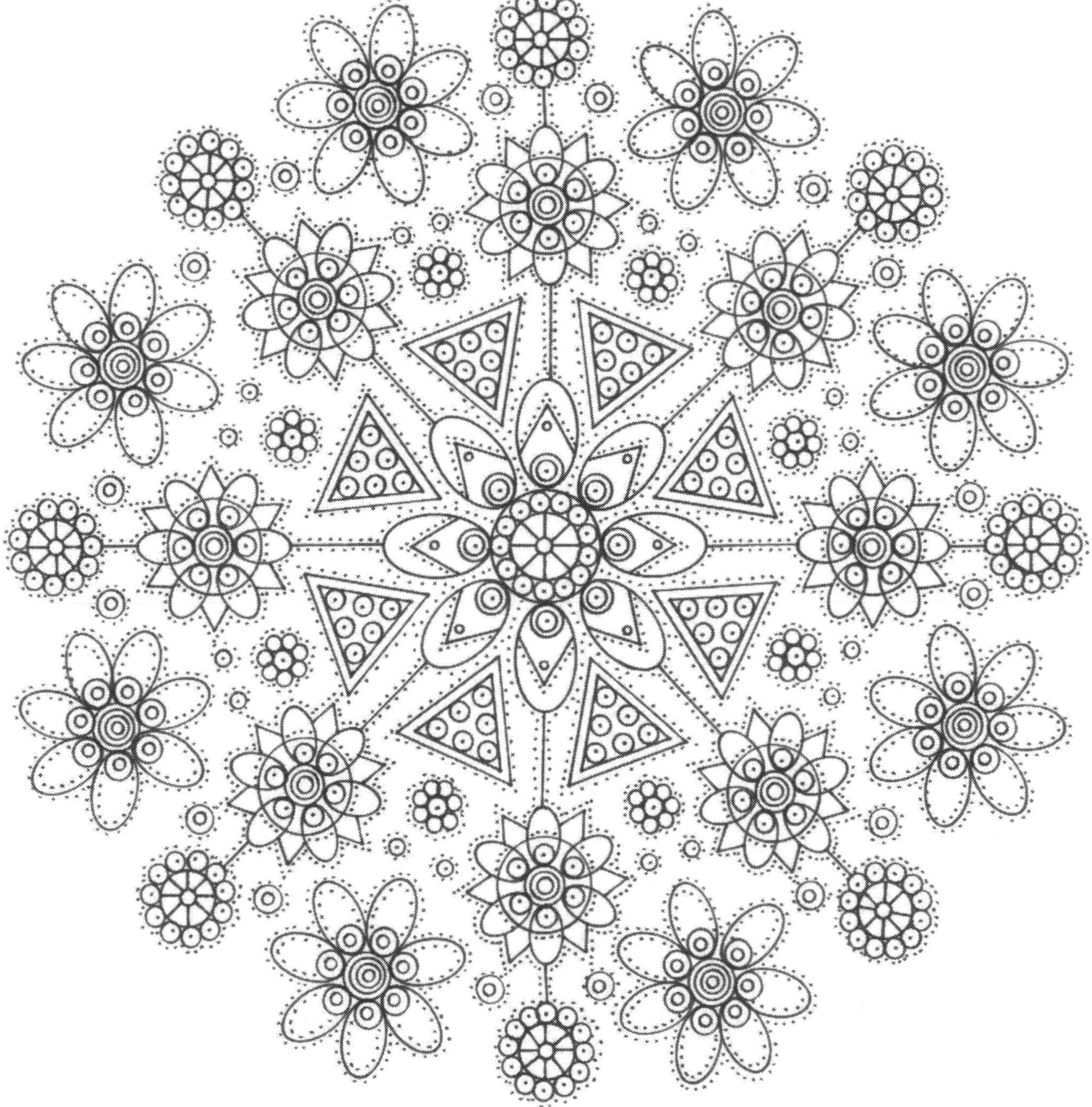

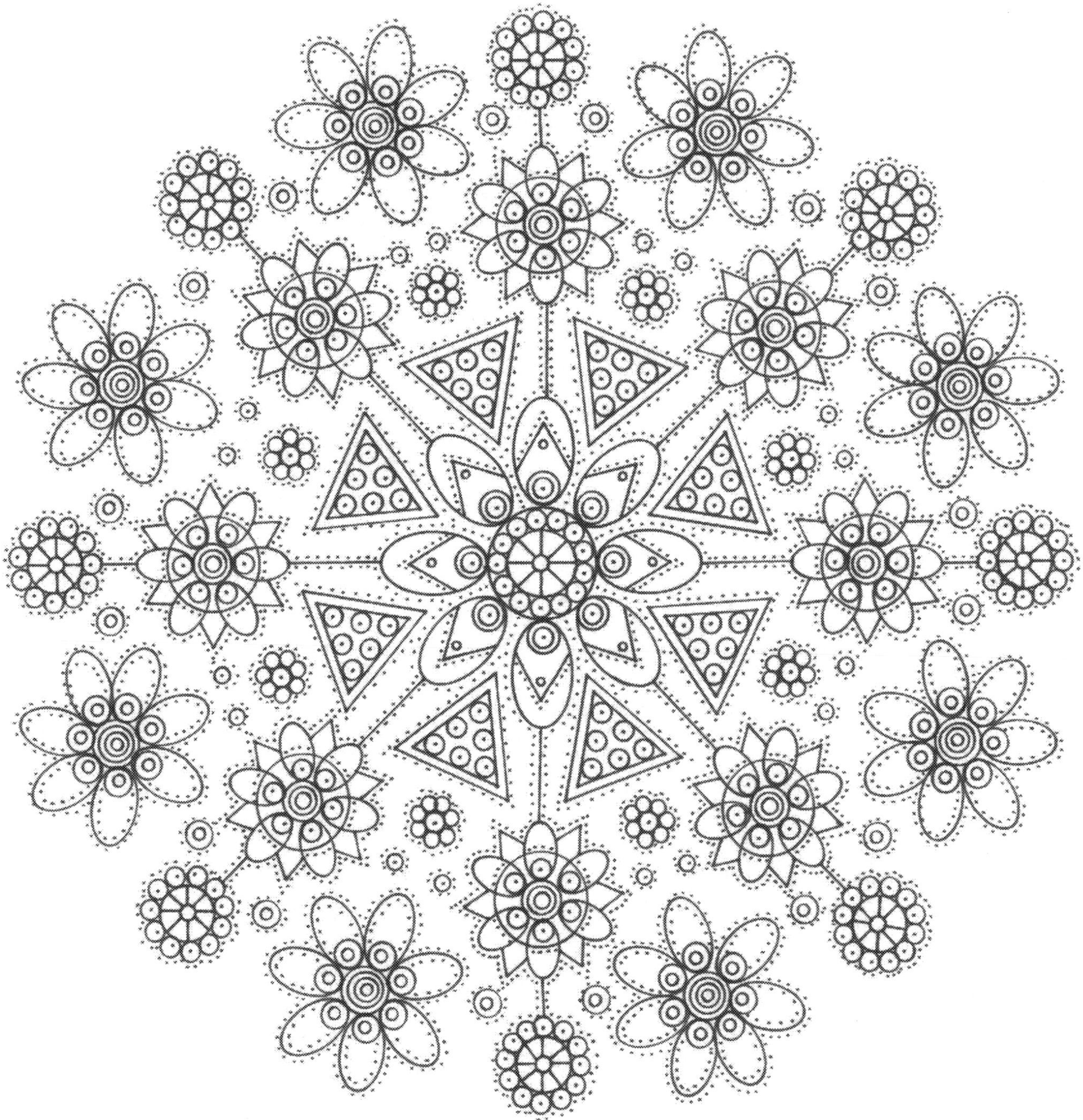

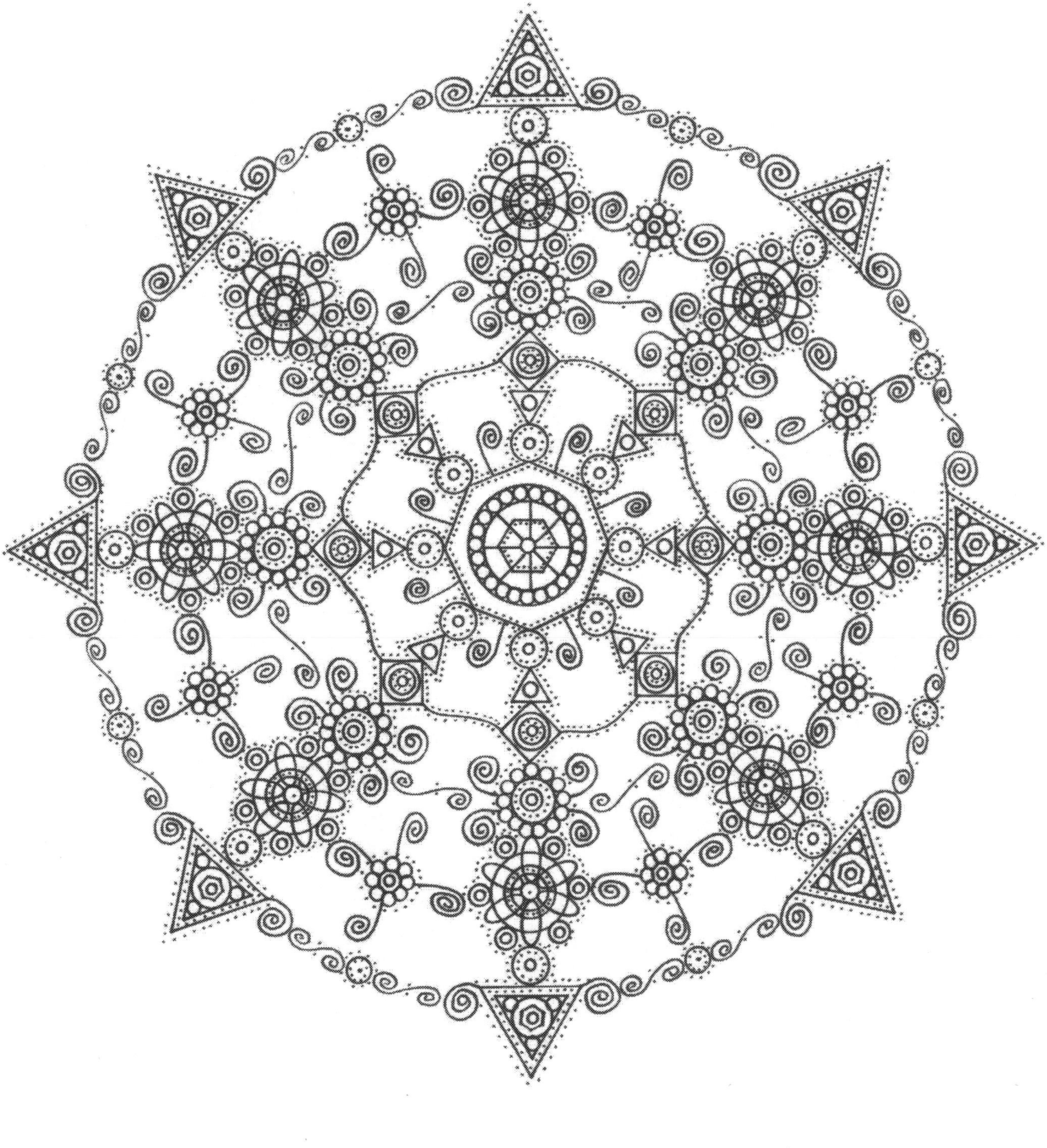

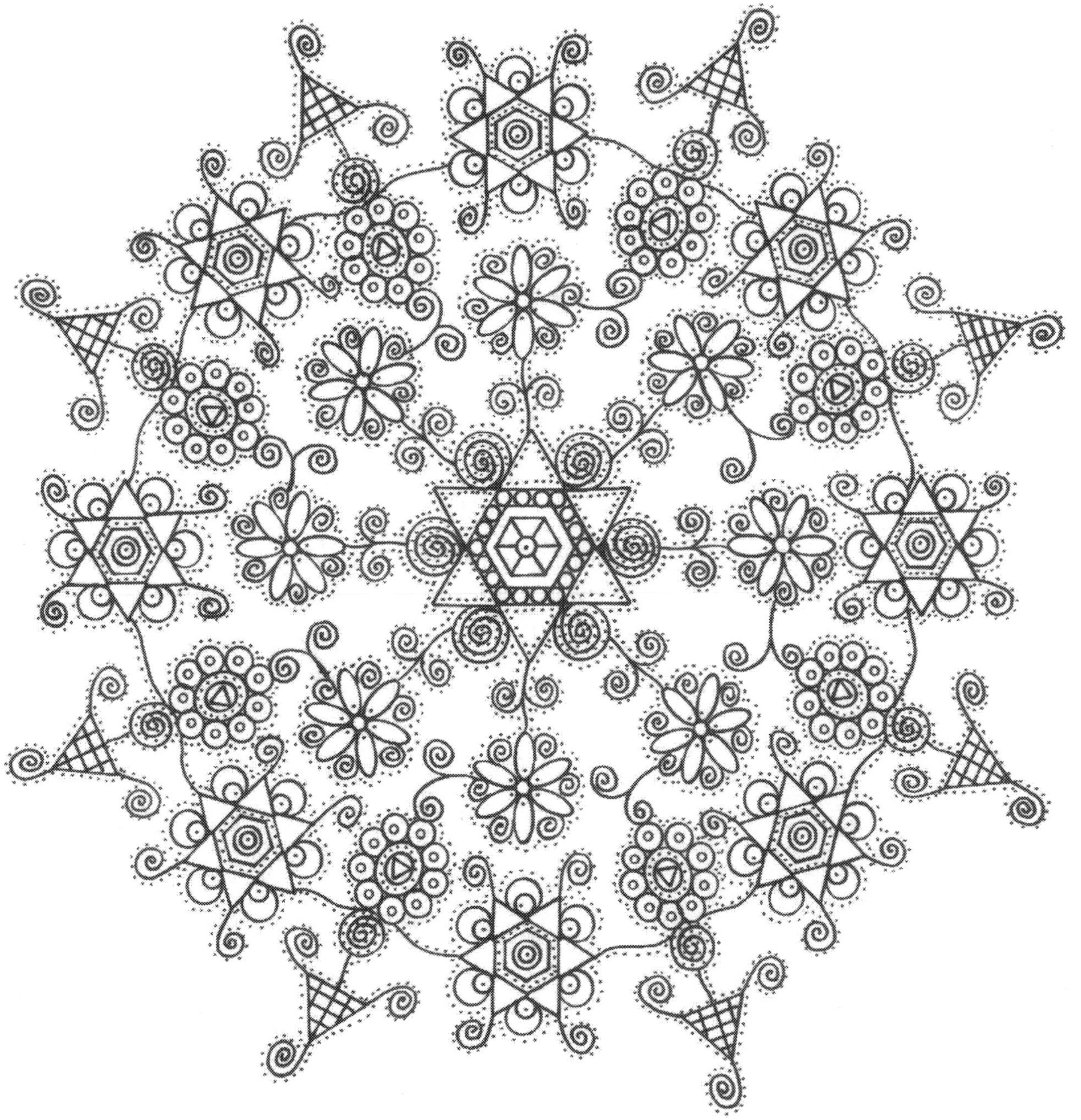

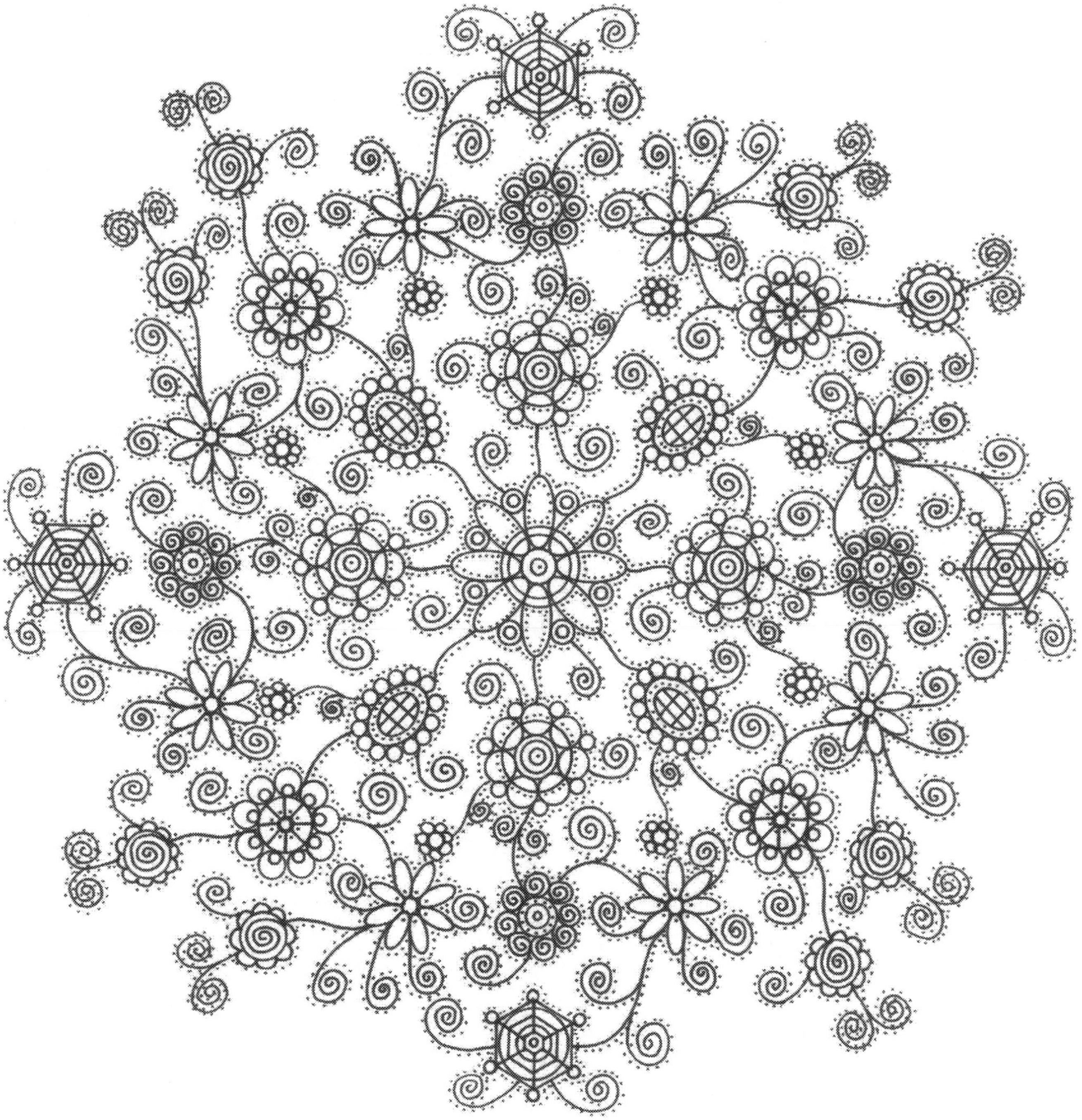

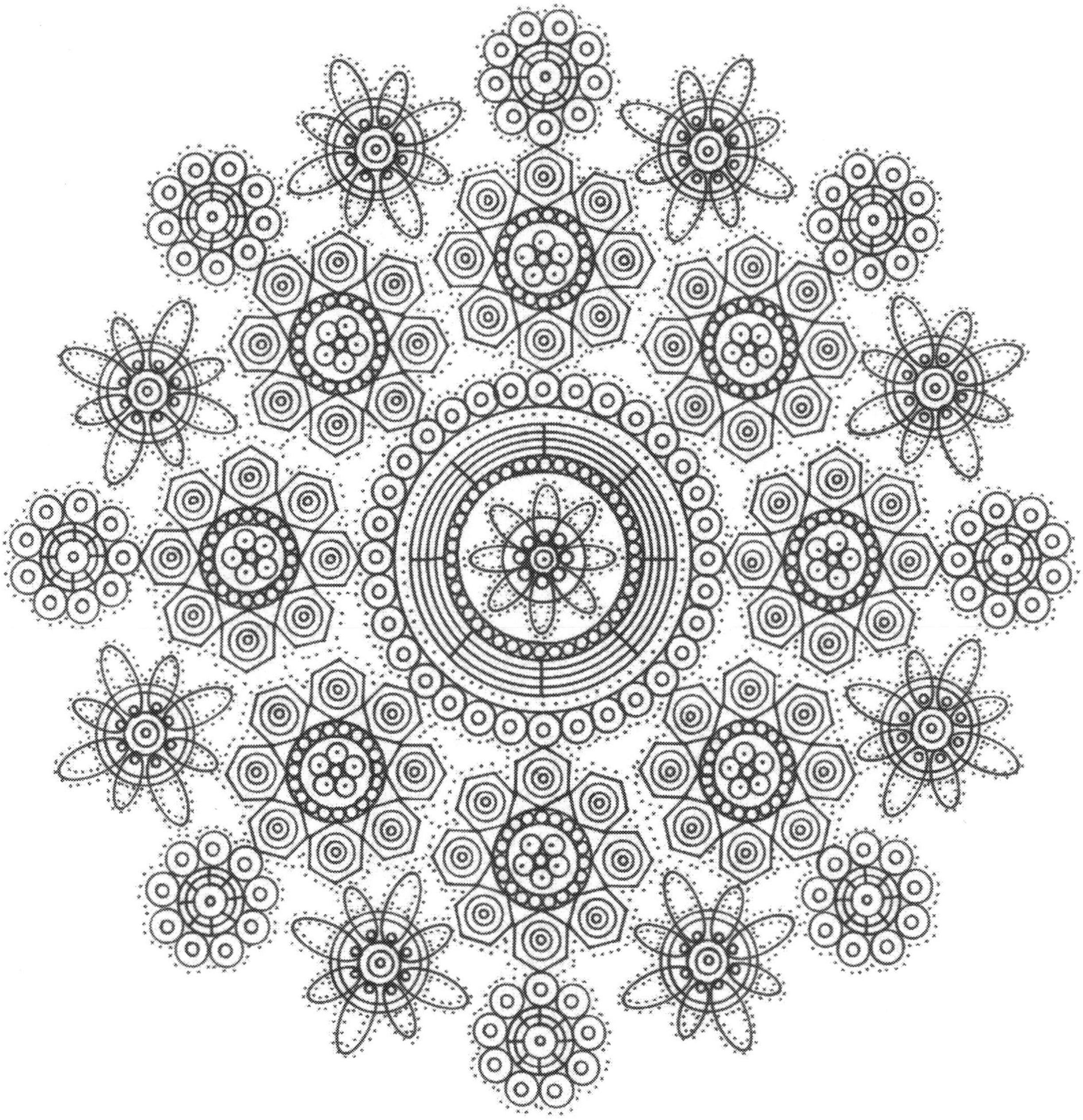

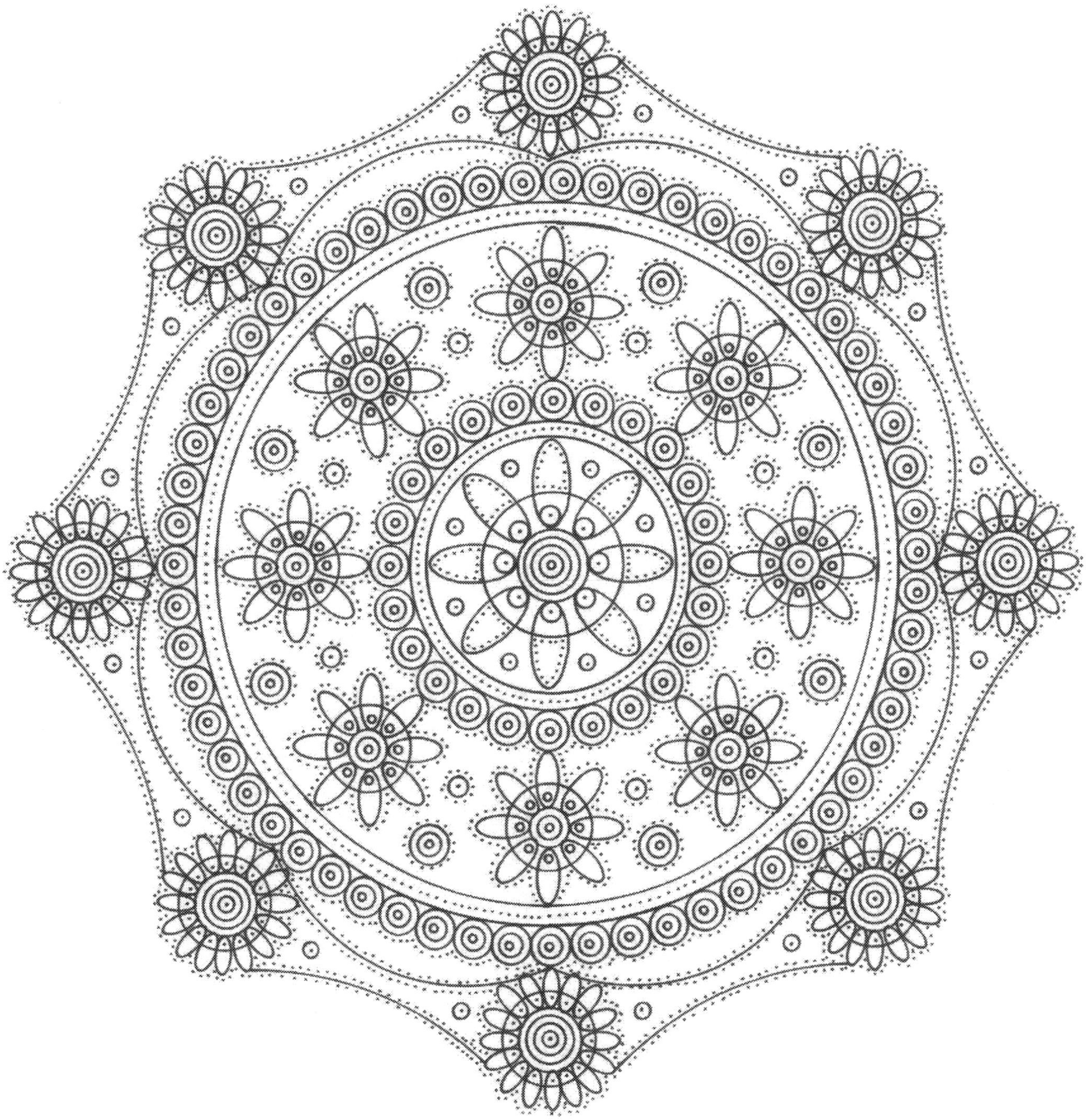

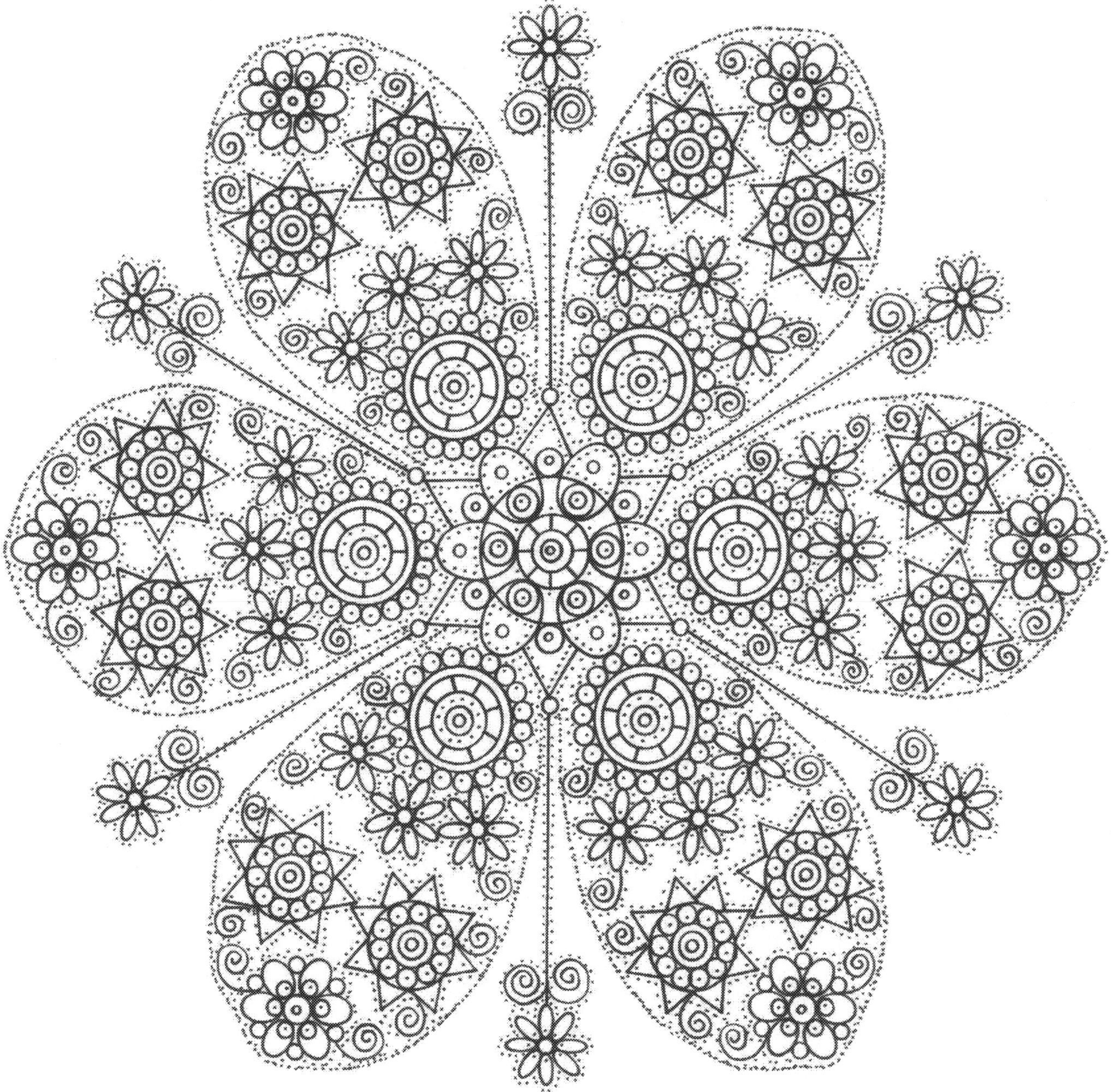

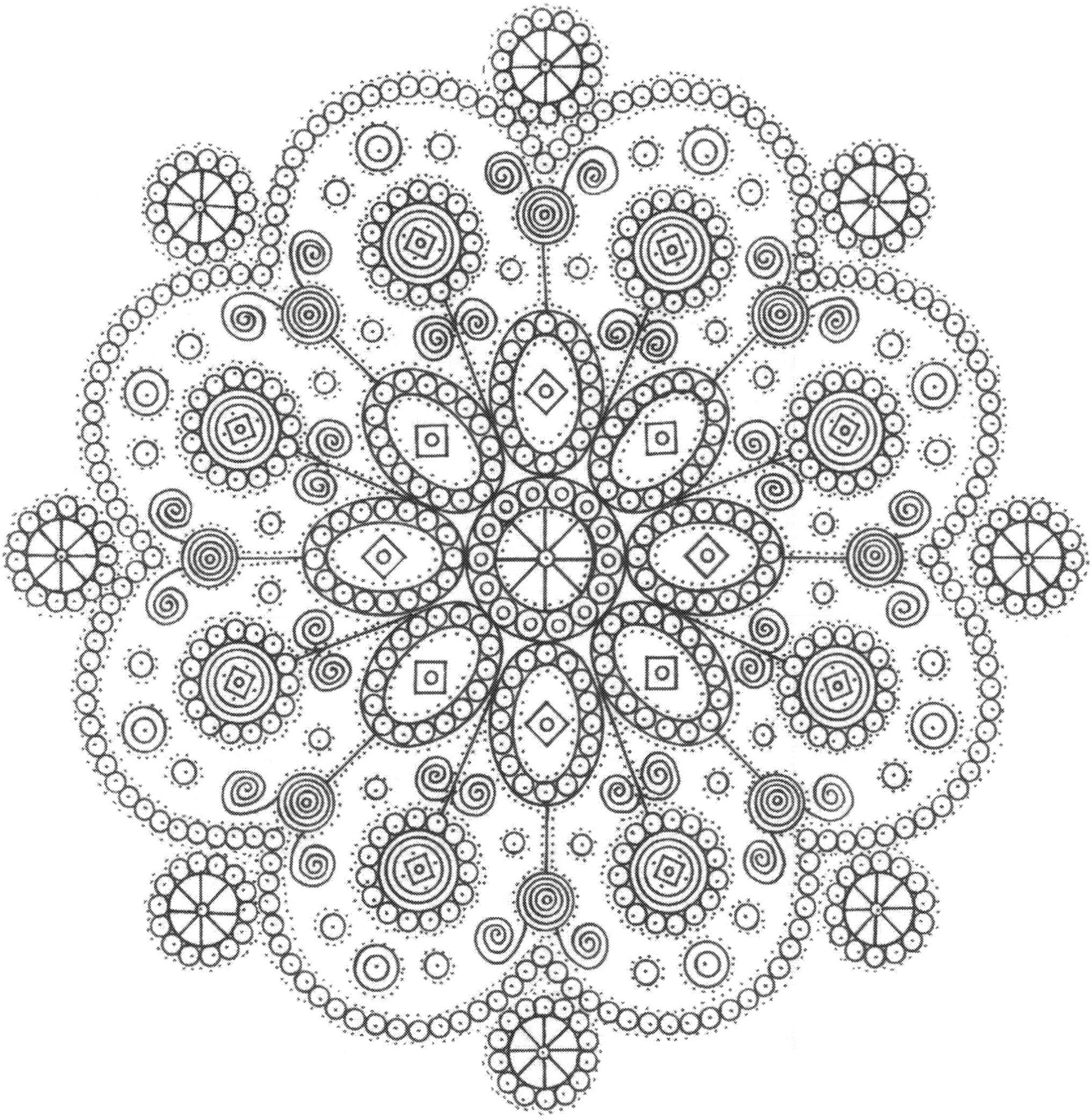

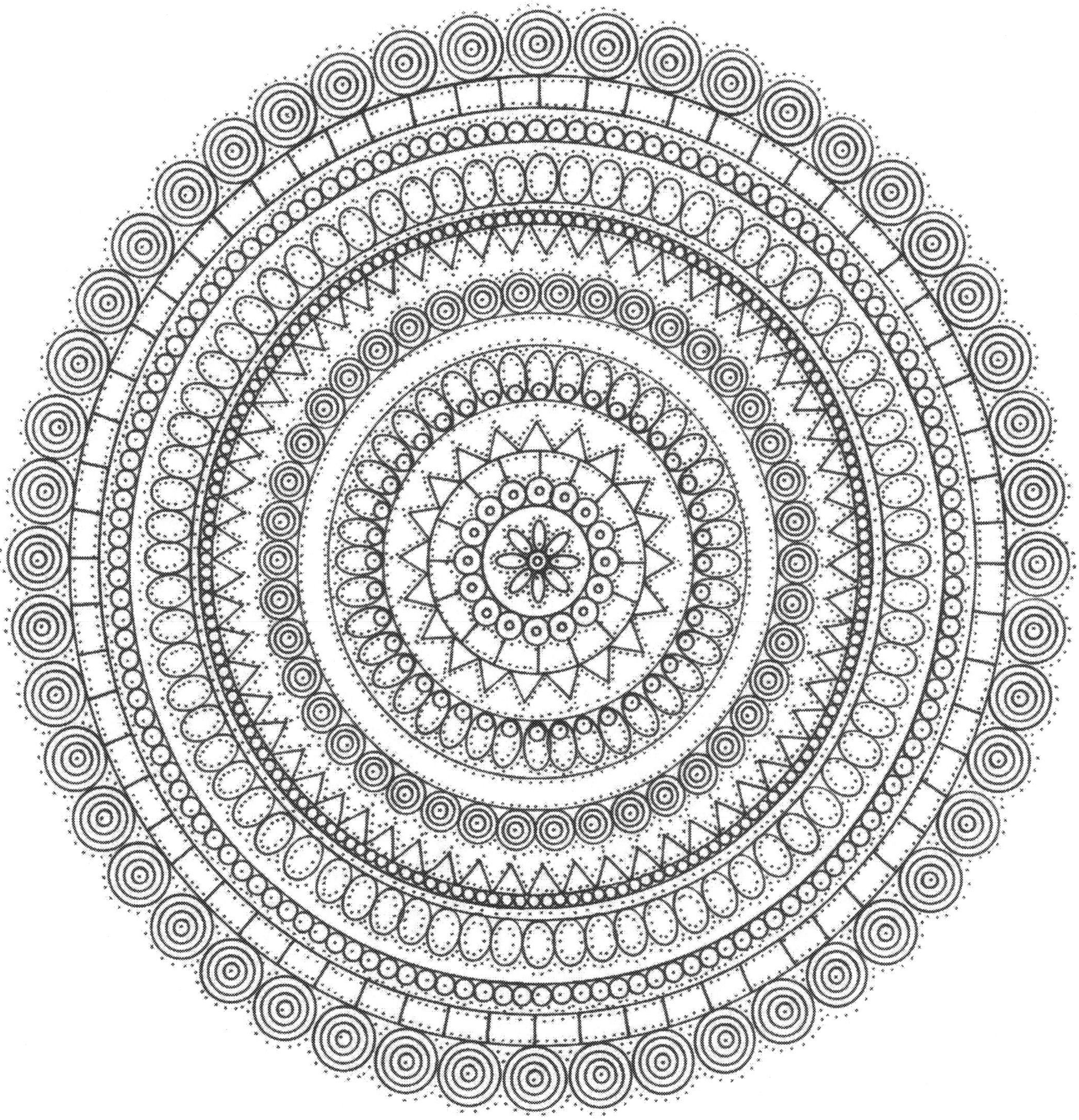

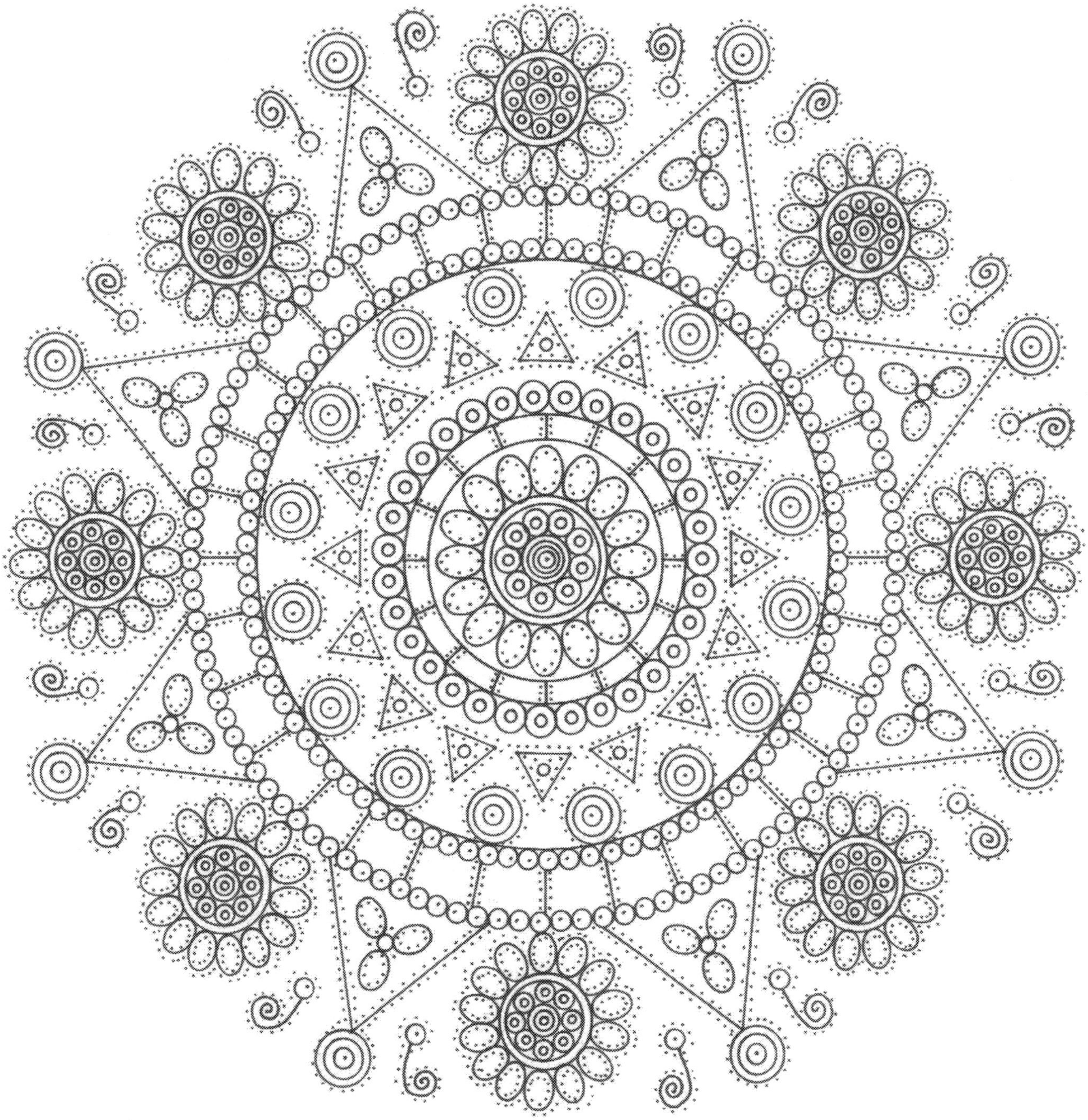

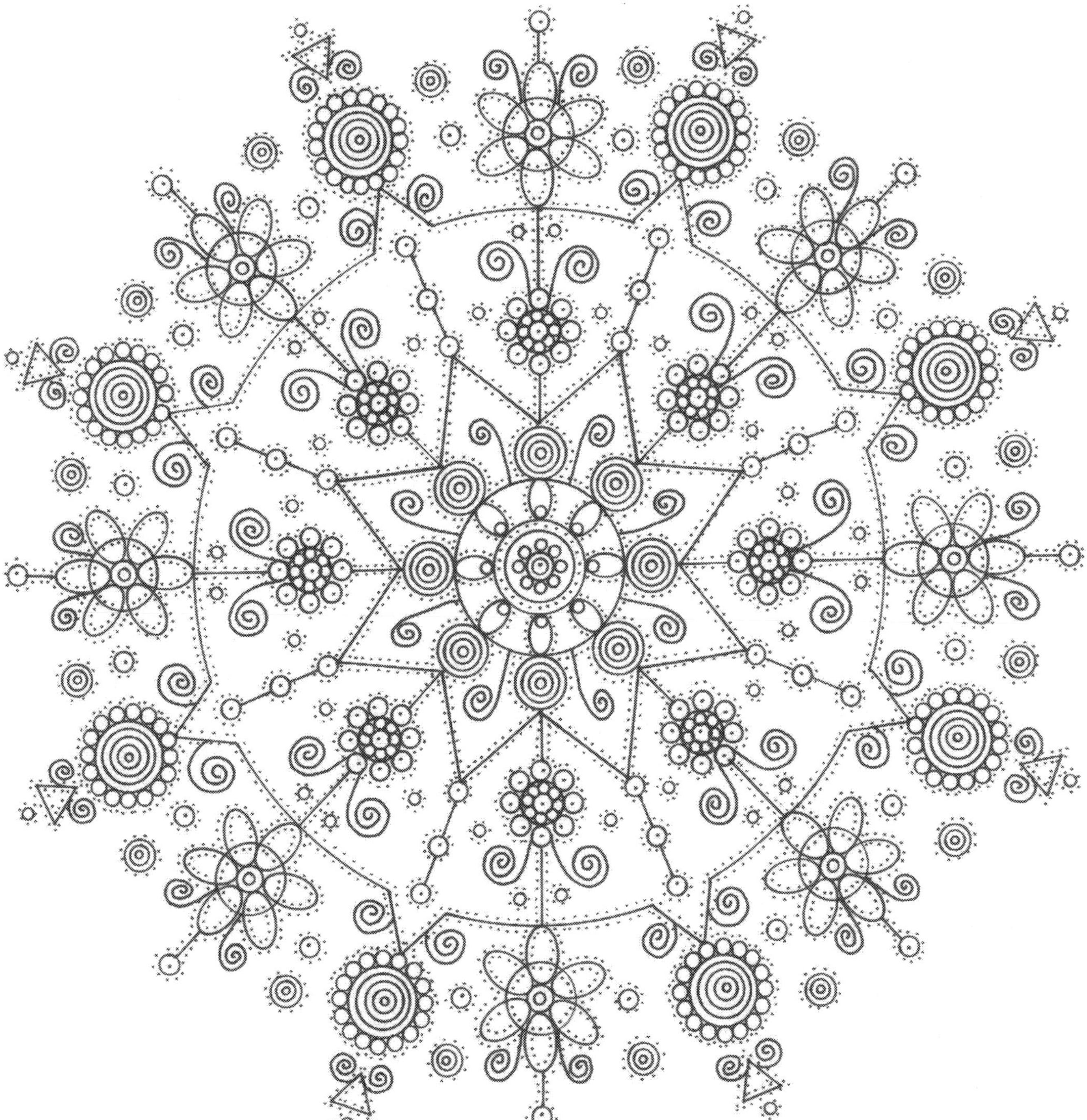

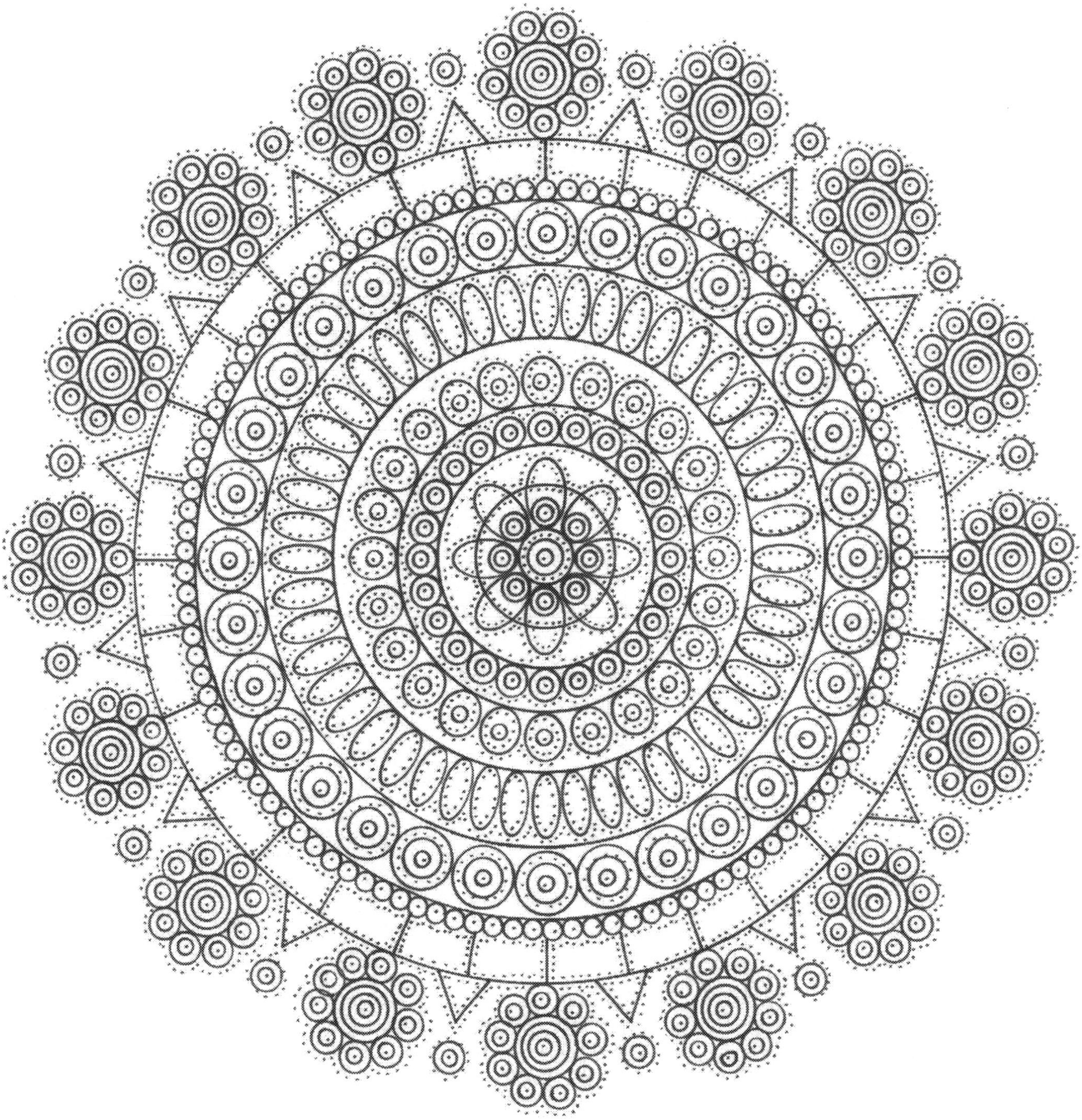

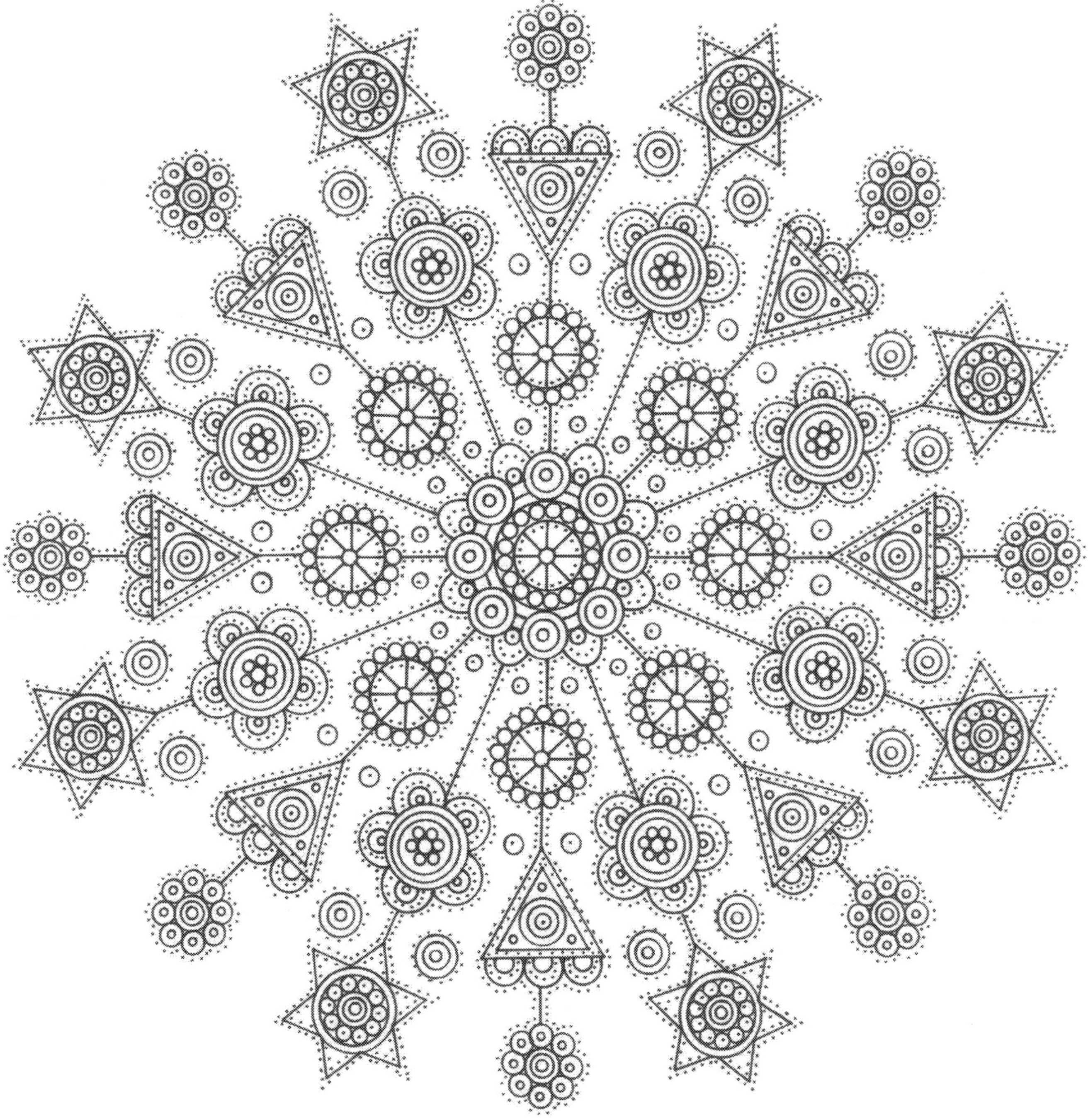

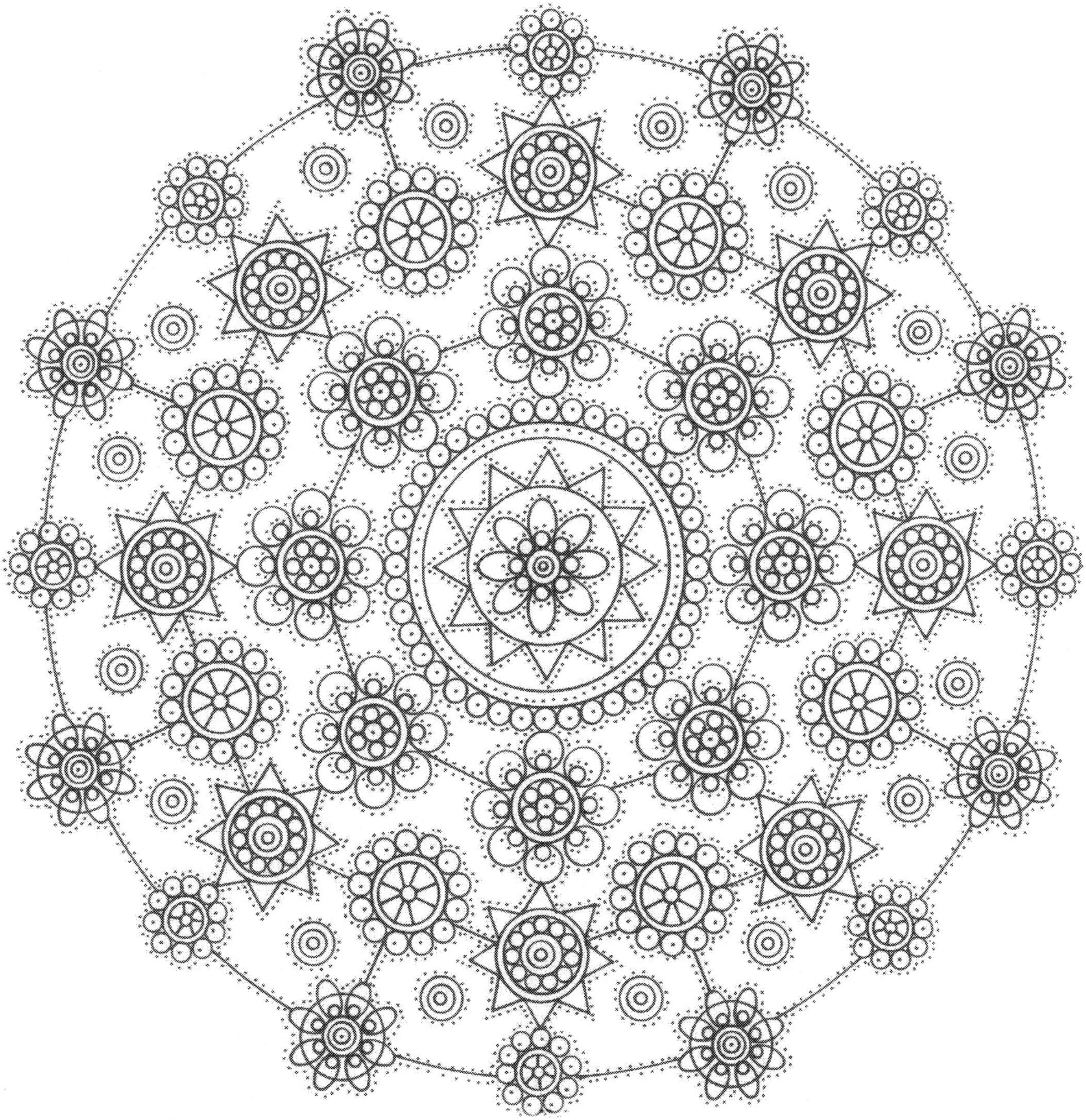

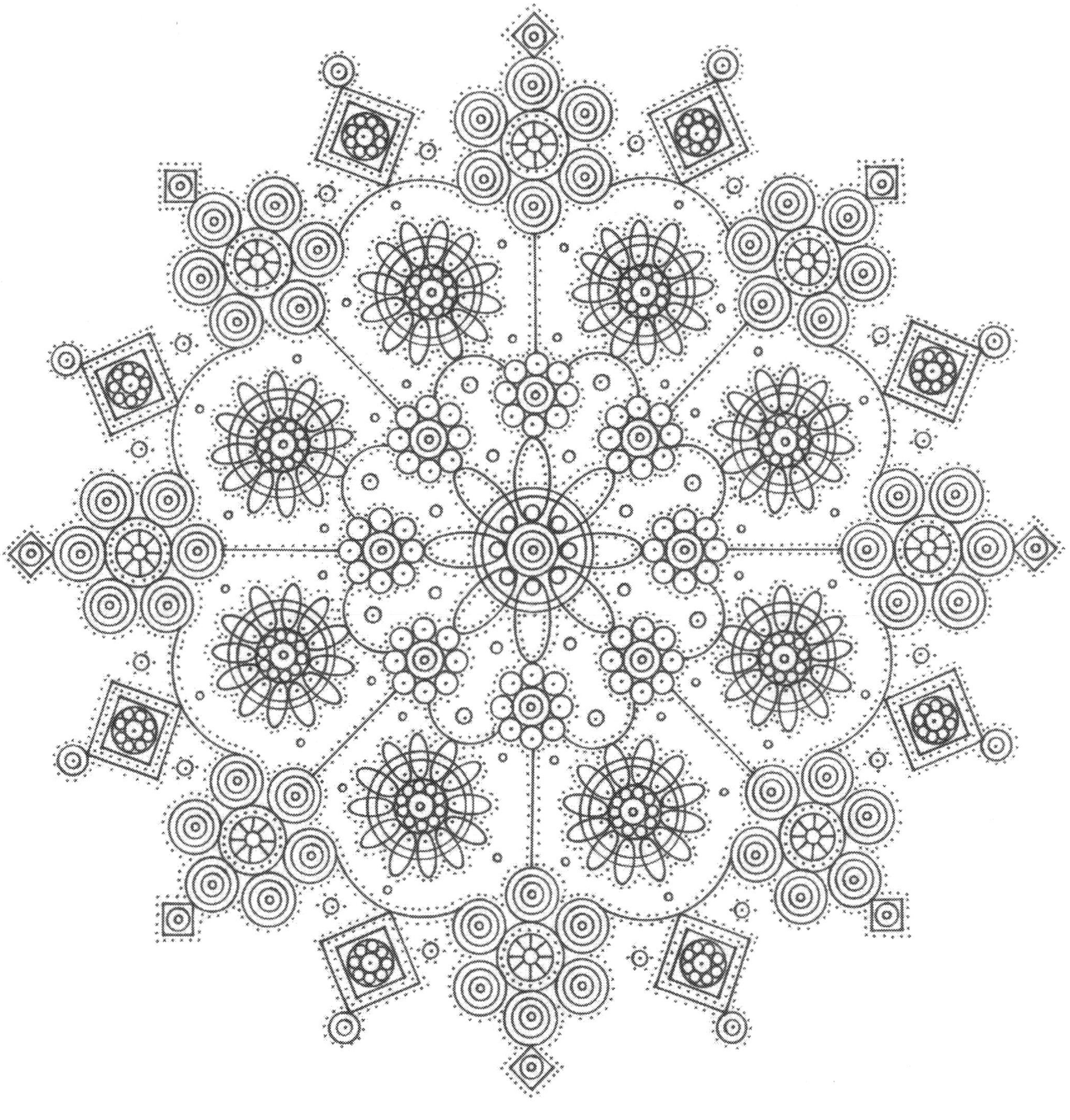

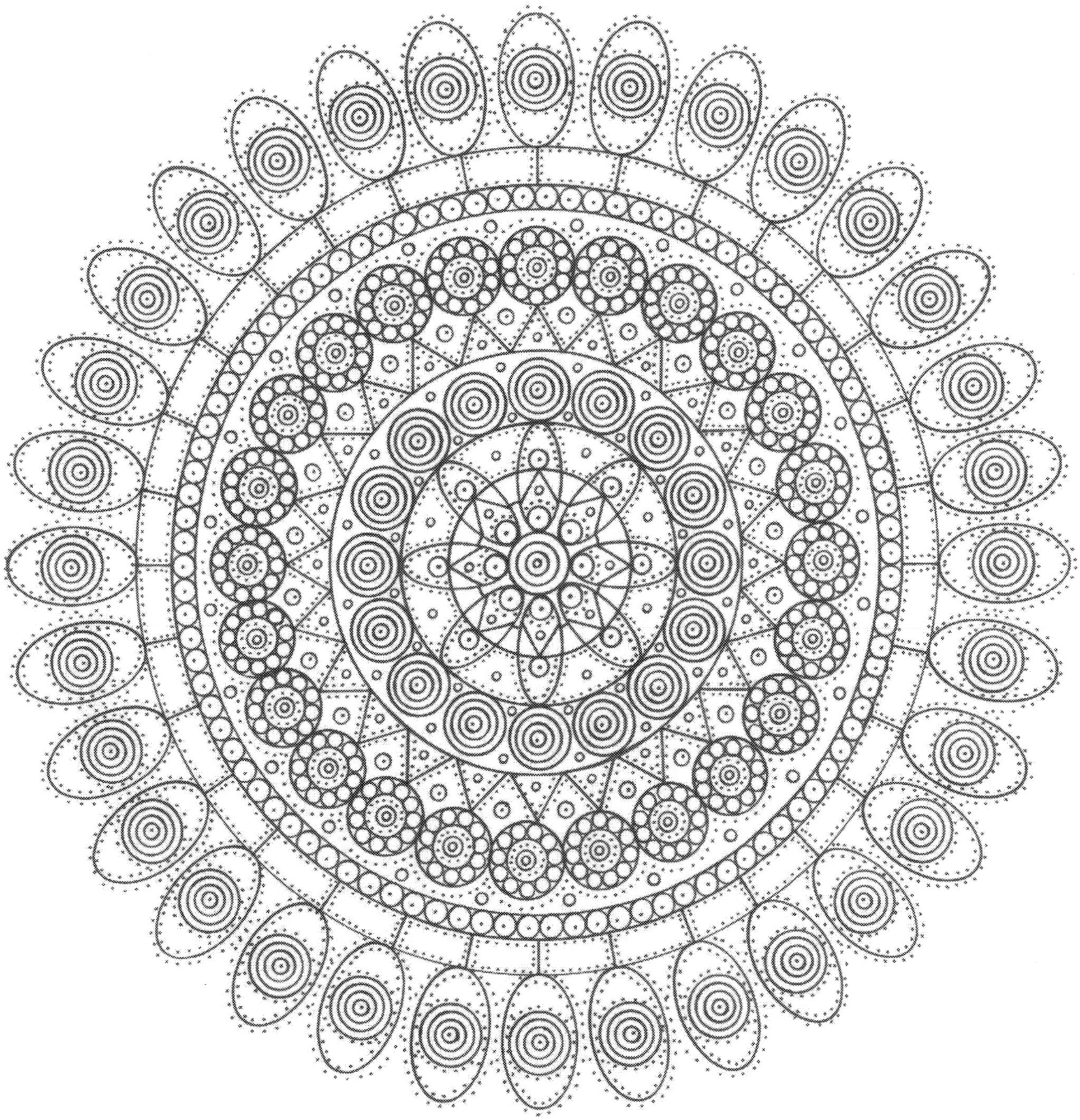

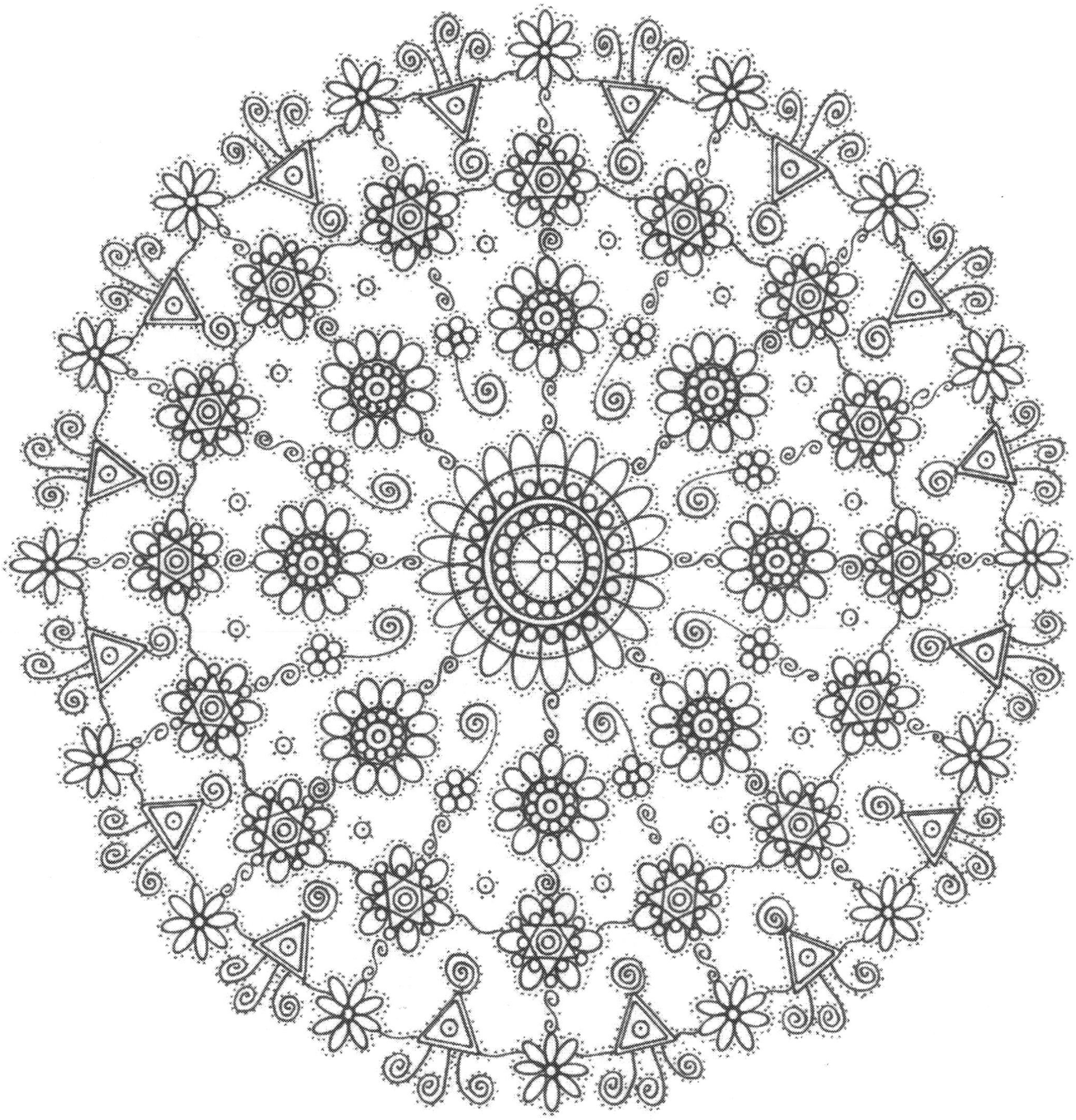

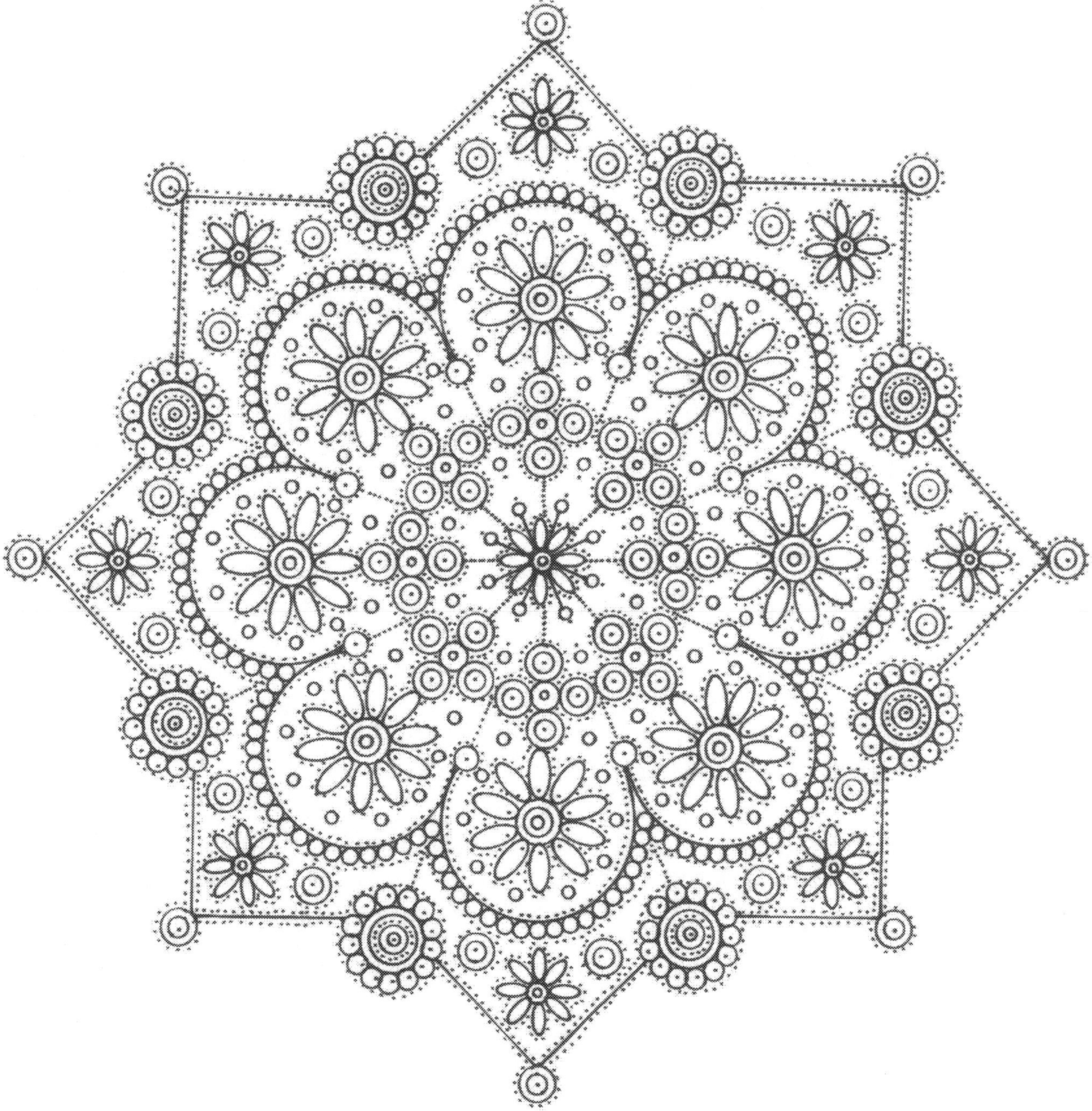

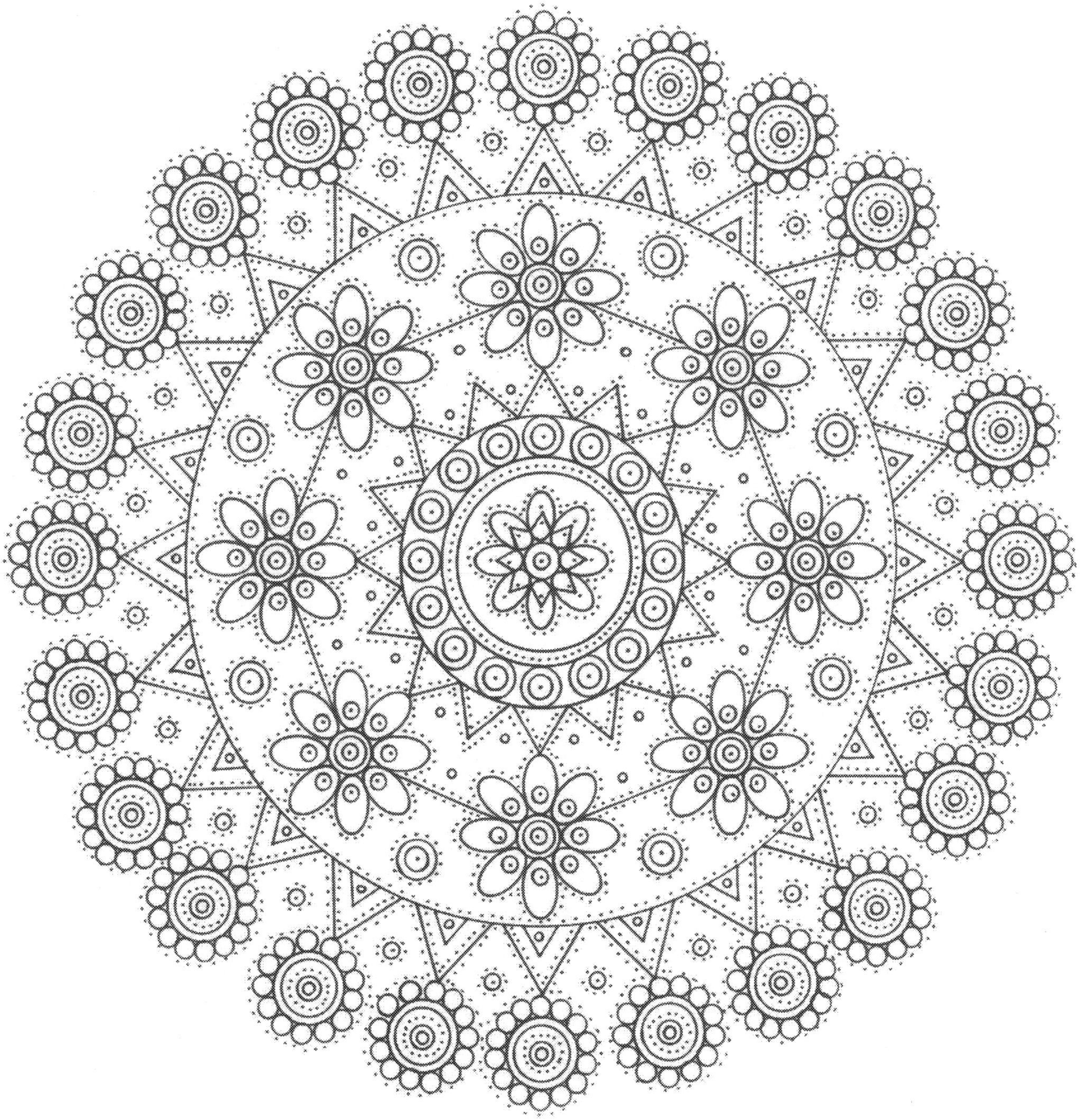

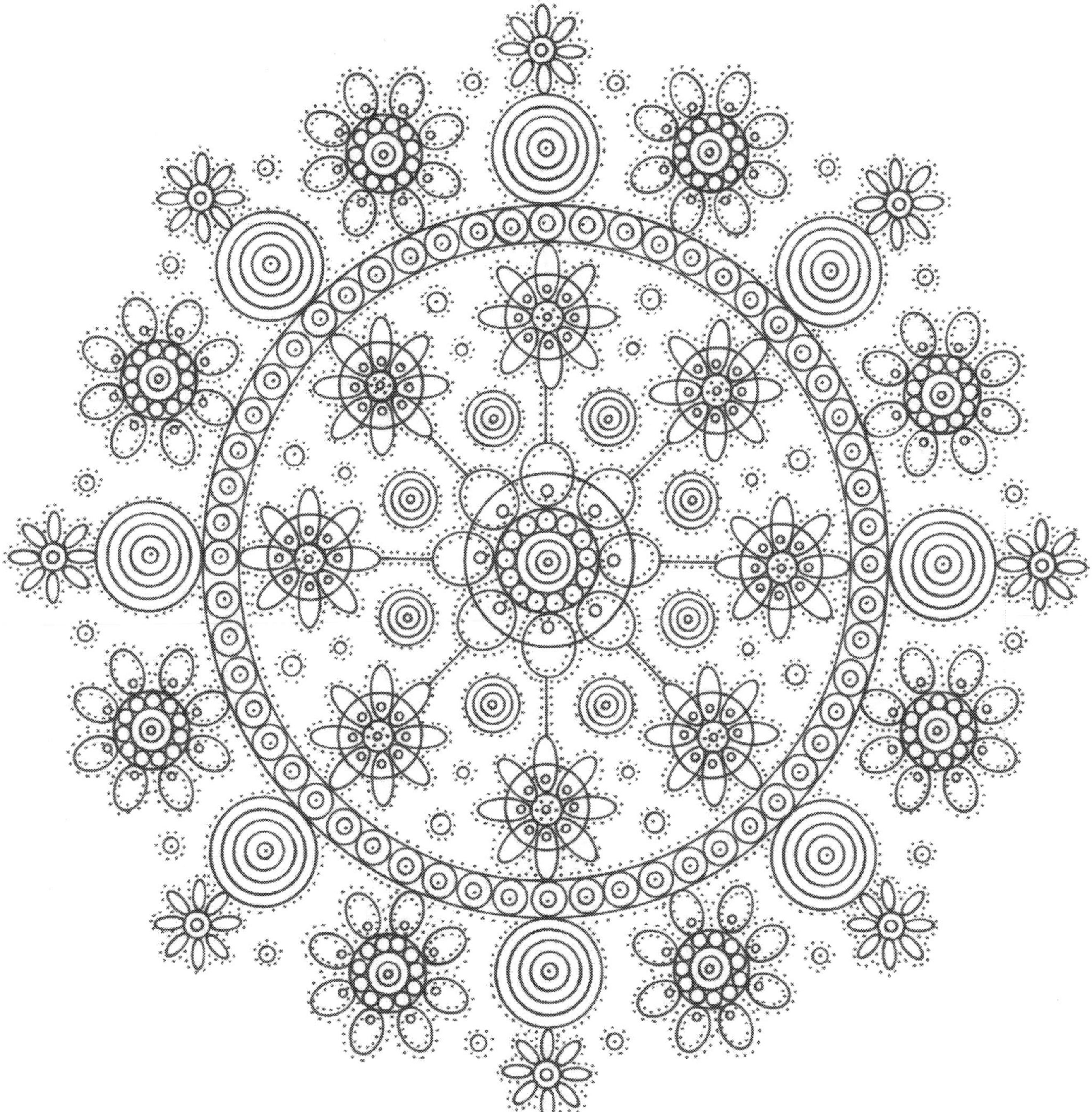

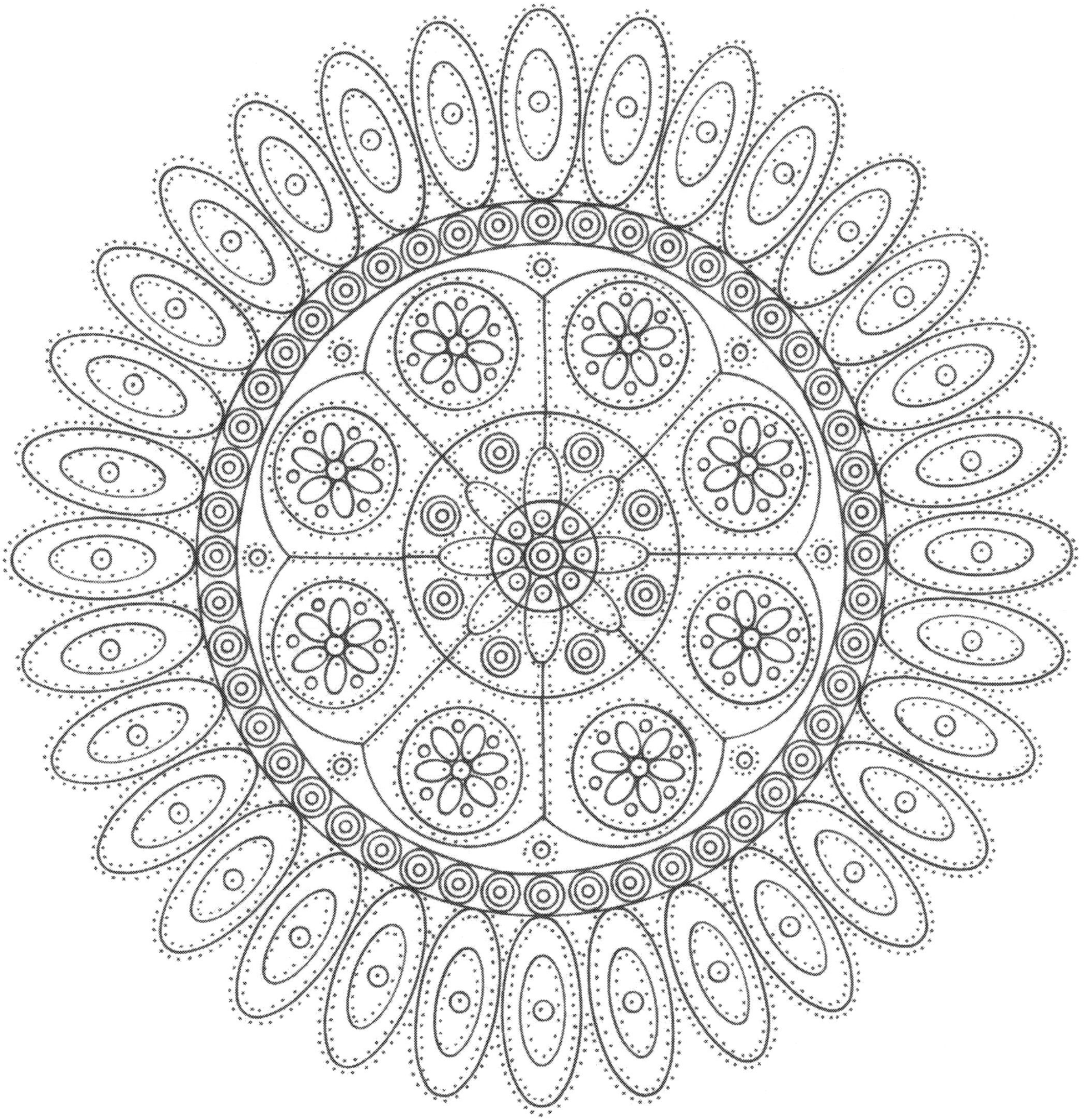

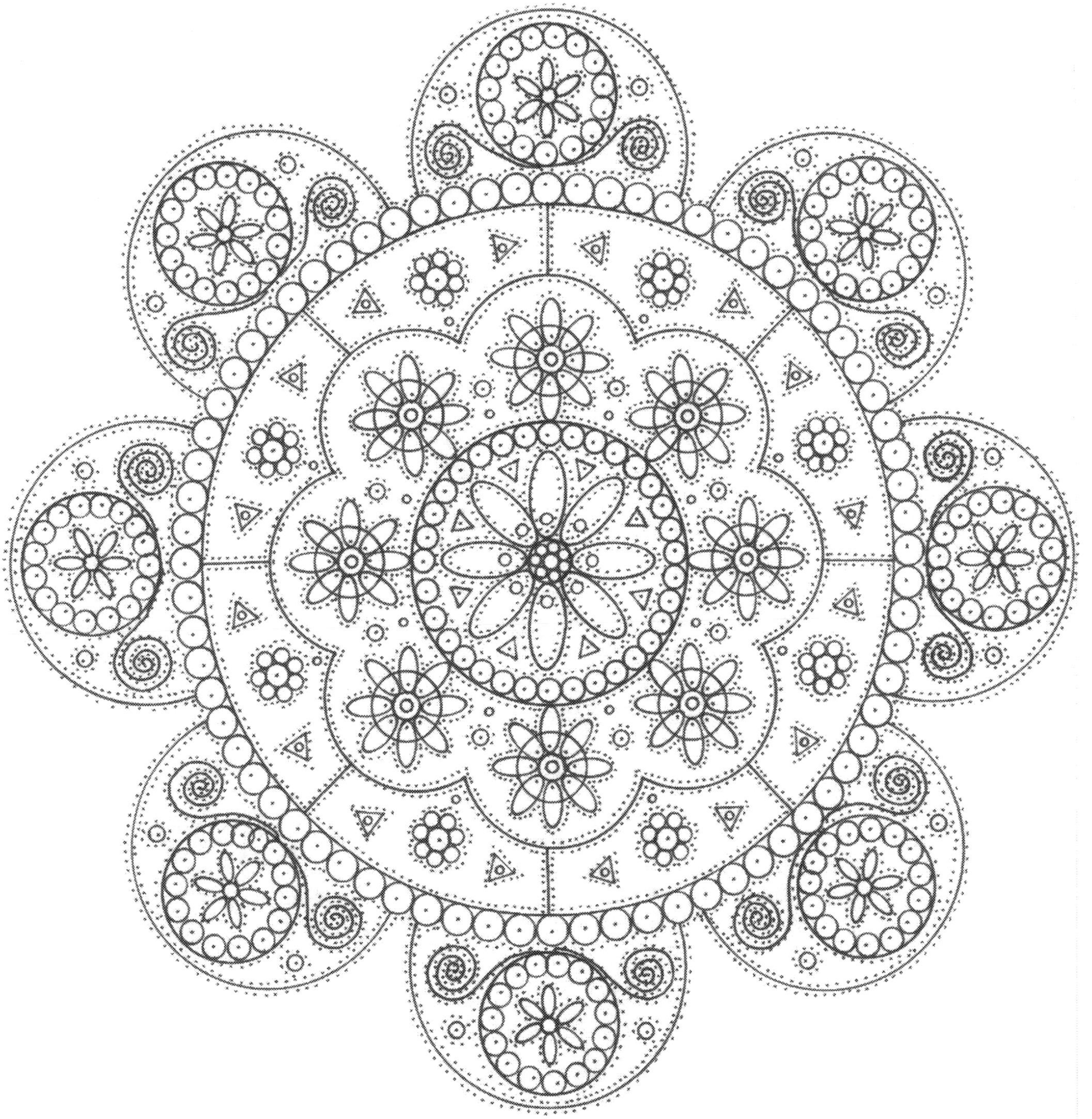

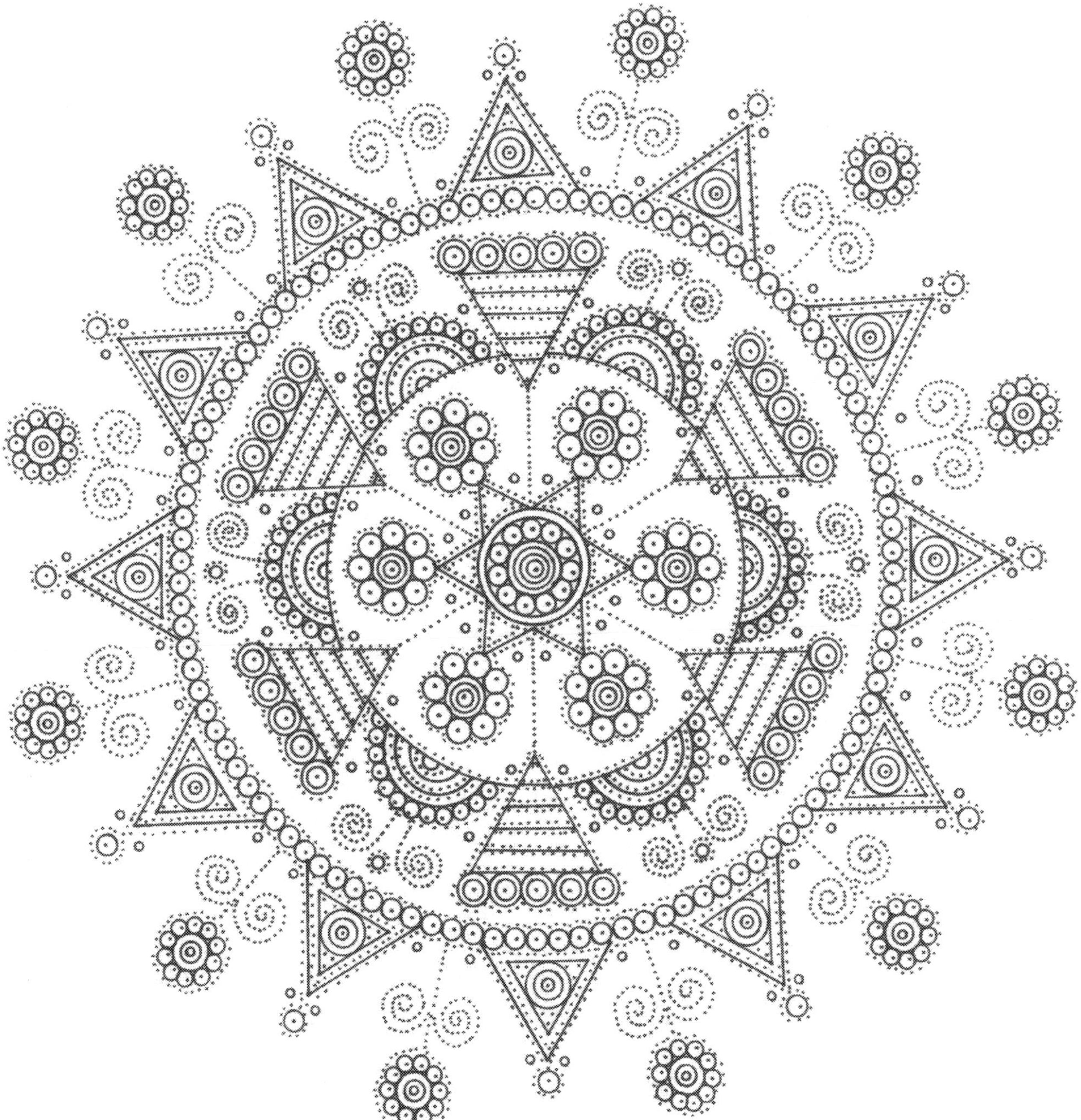

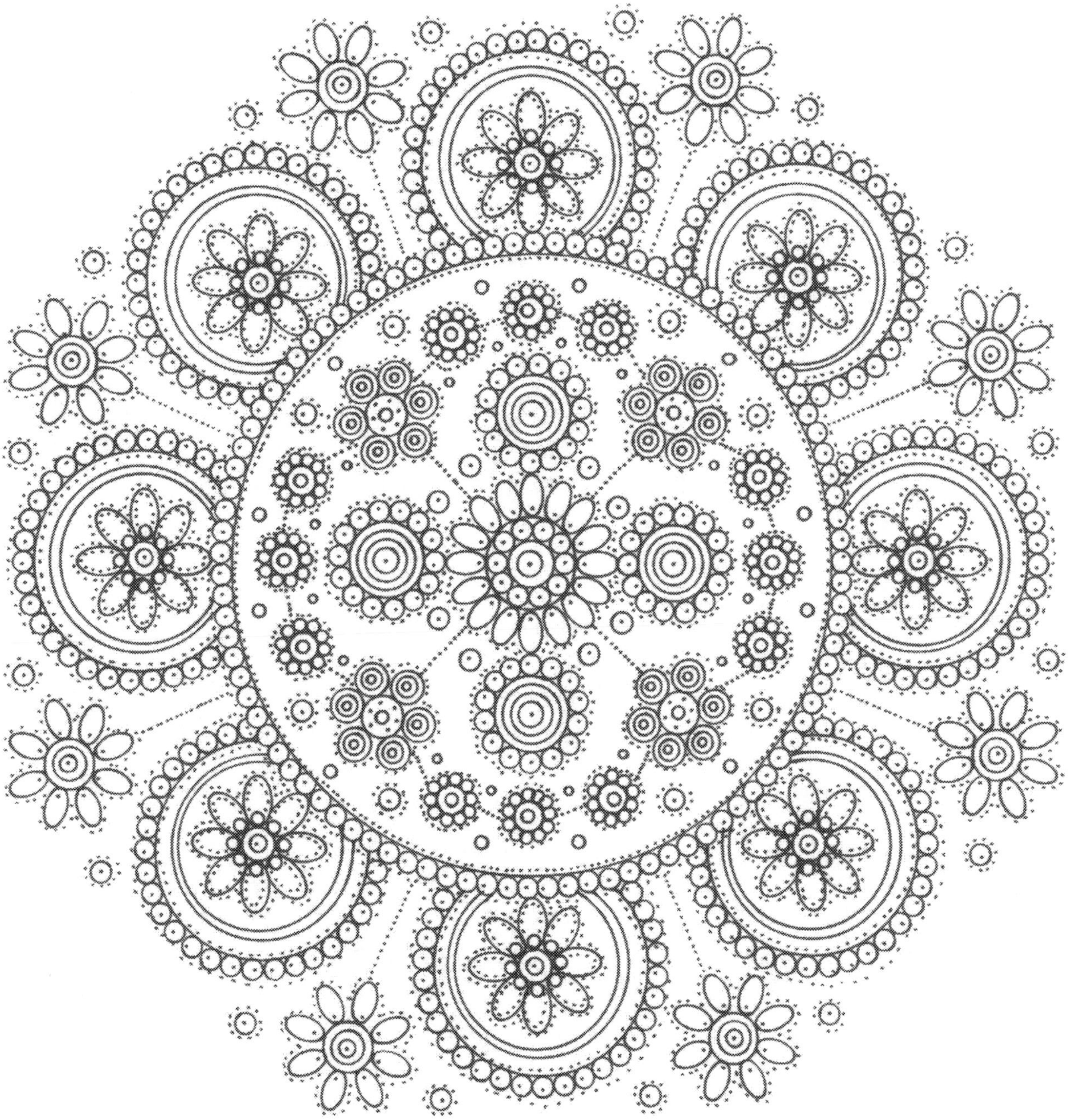